Seventh Workshop on Syntax, Semantics and Structure in Statistical Translation 2013

(SSST-7)

Atlanta, Georgia, USA
13 June 2013

Editors:

Marine Carpuat
Lucia Specia
Dekai Wu

ISBN: 978-1-62748-985-0

Printed from e-media with permission by:

Curran Associates, Inc.
57 Morehouse Lane
Red Hook, NY 12571

CURRAN ASSOCIATES INC. proceedings.com

Some format issues inherent in the e-media version may also appear in this print version.

Printed by Curran Associates, Inc. (2013)

Association for Computational Linguistics
209 N. Eighth Street
Stroudsburg, Pennsylvania 18360

Phone: 1-570-476-8006
Fax: 1-570-476-0860

acl@aclweb.org

Additional copies of this publication are available from:

Curran Associates, Inc.
57 Morehouse Lane
Red Hook, NY 12571 USA
Phone: 845-758-0400
Fax: 845-758-2634
Email: curran@proceedings.com
Web: www.proceedings.com

Introduction

The Seventh Workshop on Syntax, Semantics and Structure in Statistical Translation (SSST-7) was held on 13 June 2013 following the NAACL 2013 conference in Atlanta, GA, USA. Like the first six SSST workshops in 2007, 2008, 2009, 2010, 2011 and 2012, it aimed to bring together researchers from different communities working in the rapidly growing field of structured statistical models of natural language translation.

We selected 8 papers for this year's workshop, many of which reflect statistical machine translation's movement toward not only tree-structured and syntactic models incorporating stochastic synchronous/transduction grammars, but also increasingly semantic models and the closely linked issues of deep syntax and shallow semantics.

In the third year since "Semantics" was explicitly added to the workshop name, the work exploring SMT's connections to semantics has continued to grow. Carpuat shows that word sense disambiguation tasks can be viewed as a method for semantic evaluation of machine translation lexical choice. Singh studies the impact of the orthographic representation of Manipuri, a Sino-Tibetan language on the task of SMT to and from English, and explores its impact on lexical ambiguity.

Several papers deepen our understanding of theoretical and practical issues associated with structured statistical translation models.

Maillette de Buy Wenniger and Sima'an show how to extend rules in a hierarchical phrase-based system with reordering information, by defining more specific nonterminals and augmenting rules with features. Huck, Vilar, Freitag and Ney present a detailed empirical study of cube pruning for hierarchical phrase-based systems. Herrmann, Niehues and Waibel incorporate a syntactic tree-based reordering method to model long-range reorderings in a phrase-based machine translation system, and combine reordering models at different levels of linguistic representation.

Saers, Addanki and Wu present an unsupervised method for inducing an Inversion Transduction Grammar based on the Minimum Description Length principle. Maillette de Buy Wenniger and Sima'an propose a precise definition of what it means for an Inversion Transduction Grammar to cover the word alignment of a sentence, and experiment with human and machine-made alignments. Kaeshammer explores the expressiveness of synchronous linear context-free rewriting systems for machine translation by computing derivation coverage on manually word aligned parallel text.

Thanks are due once again to our authors and our Program Committee for making the seventh SSST workshop another success.

Marine Carpuat, Lucia Specia, and Dekai Wu

Organizers:

Marine Carpuat, National Research Council Canada
Lucia Specia, University of Sheffield
Dekai Wu, Hong Kong University of Science and Technology

Program Committee:

Marianna Apidianak, LIMSI-CNRS
Wilker Aziz, University of Wolverhampton
Srinivas Bangalore, AT&T Labs Research
Yee Seng Chan, Raytheon BBN Technologies
Colin Cherry, National Research Council Canada
David Chiang, USC/ISI
John DeNero, Google
Marc Dymetman, Xerox Research Centre Europe
Alexander Fraser, Universität Stuttgart
Daniel Gildea, University of Rochester
Greg Hanneman, Carnegie Mellon University
Yifan He, New York University
Hieu Hoang, University of Edinburgh
Philipp Koehn, University of Edinburgh
Els Lefever, Hogeschool Gent
Chi-kiu Lo, HKUST
Daniel Marcu, SDL
Aurélien Max, LIMSI-CNRS & Univ. Paris Sud
Daniele Pighin, Google
Markus Saers, HKUST
Taro Watanabe, NICT
Deyi Xiong, Institute for Infocomm Research
Bowen Zhou, IBM Research

Table of Contents

A Semantic Evaluation of Machine Translation Lexical Choice
Marine Carpuat 1

Taste of Two Different Flavours: Which Manipuri Script works better for English-Manipuri Language pair SMT Systems?
Thoudam Doren Singh 11

Hierarchical Alignment Decomposition Labels for Hiero Grammar Rules
Gideon Maillette de Buy Wenniger and Khalil Sima'an 19

A Performance Study of Cube Pruning for Large-Scale Hierarchical Machine Translation
Matthias Huck, David Vilar, Markus Freitag and Hermann Ney 29

Combining Word Reordering Methods on different Linguistic Abstraction Levels for Statistical Machine Translation
Teresa Herrmann, Jan Niehues and Alex Waibel 39

Combining Top-down and Bottom-up Search for Unsupervised Induction of Transduction Grammars
Markus Saers, Karteek Addanki and Dekai Wu 48

A Formal Characterization of Parsing Word Alignments by Synchronous Grammars with Empirical Evidence to the ITG Hypothesis.
Gideon Maillette de Buy Wenniger and Khalil Sima'an 58

Synchronous Linear Context-Free Rewriting Systems for Machine Translation
Miriam Kaeshammer 68

Conference Program

Thursday, June 13, 2013

9:15–9:30 Opening Remarks

Session 1

9:30–10:00 *A Semantic Evaluation of Machine Translation Lexical Choice*
Marine Carpuat

10:00–10:30 *Taste of Two Different Flavours: Which Manipuri Script works better for English-Manipuri Language pair SMT Systems?*
Thoudam Doren Singh

10:30–11:00 Break

Session 2

11:00–11:30 *Hierarchical Alignment Decomposition Labels for Hiero Grammar Rules*
Gideon Maillette de Buy Wenniger and Khalil Sima'an

11:30–12:00 *A Performance Study of Cube Pruning for Large-Scale Hierarchical Machine Translation*
Matthias Huck, David Vilar, Markus Freitag and Hermann Ney

12:00–12:30 *Combining Word Reordering Methods on different Linguistic Abstraction Levels for Statistical Machine Translation*
Teresa Herrmann, Jan Niehues and Alex Waibel

12:30–2:00 Lunch

Thursday, June 13, 2013 (continued)

Session 3

2:00–3:00 Panel discussion: Meaning Representations for Machine Translation, with Jan Hajic, Kevin Knight, Martha Palmer and Dekai Wu

3:30–4:00 *Combining Top-down and Bottom-up Search for Unsupervised Induction of Transduction Grammars*
Markus Saers, Karteek Addanki and Dekai Wu

3:30–4:00 Break

Session 4

4:00–4:30 *A Formal Characterization of Parsing Word Alignments by Synchronous Grammars with Empirical Evidence to the ITG Hypothesis.*
Gideon Maillette de Buy Wenniger and Khalil Sima'an

4:30–5:00 *Synchronous Linear Context-Free Rewriting Systems for Machine Translation*
Miriam Kaeshammer

A Semantic Evaluation of Machine Translation Lexical Choice

Marine Carpuat
National Research Council Canada
1200 Montreal Rd,
Ottawa, ON K1A 0R6
Marine.Carpuat@nrc.gc.ca

Abstract

While automatic metrics of translation quality are invaluable for machine translation research, deeper understanding of translation errors require more focused evaluations designed to target specific aspects of translation quality. We show that Word Sense Disambiguation (WSD) can be used to evaluate the quality of machine translation lexical choice, by applying a standard phrase-based SMT system on the SemEval2010 Cross-Lingual WSD task. This case study reveals that the SMT system does not perform as well as a WSD system trained on the exact same parallel data, and that local context models based on source phrases and target n-grams are much weaker representations of context than the simple templates used by the WSD system.

1 Introduction

Much research has focused on automatically evaluating the quality of Machine Translation (MT) by comparing automatic translations to human translations on samples of a few thousand sentences. Many metrics (Papineni et al., 2002; Banerjee and Lavie, 2005; Giménez and Márquez, 2007; Lo and Wu, 2011, for instance) have been proposed to estimate the adequacy and fluency of machine translation and evaluated based on their correlatation with human judgements of translation quality (Callison-Burch et al., 2010). While these metrics have proven invaluable in driving progress in MT research, finer-grained evaluations of translation quality are necessary to provide a more focused analysis of translation errors. When developing complex MT systems, comparing BLEU or TER scores is not sufficient to understand what improved or what went wrong. Error analysis can of course be done manually (Vilar et al., 2006), but it is often too slow and expensive to be performed as often as needed during system development.

Several metrics have been recently proposed to evaluate specific aspects of translation quality such as word order (Birch et al., 2010; Chen et al., 2012). While word order is indirectly taken into account by BLEU, TER or METEOR scores, dedicated metrics provide a direct evaluation that lets us understand whether a given system's reordering performance improved during system development. Word order metrics provide a *complementary* tool for targeting evaluation and analysis to a specific aspect of machine translation quality.

There has not been as much work on evaluating the lexical choice performance of MT: does a MT system preserve the meaning of words in translation? This is of course measured indirectly by commonly used global metrics, but a more focused evaluation can help us gain a better understanding of the behavior of MT systems.

In this paper, we show that MT lexical choice can be framed and evaluated as a standard Word Sense Disambiguation (WSD) task. We leverage existing WSD shared tasks in order to evaluate whether word meaning is preserved in translation. Let us emphasize that, just like reordering metrics, our WSD evaluation is meant to *complement* global metrics of translation quality. In previous work, intrinsic evaluations of lexical choice have been performed using either semi-automatically constructed data sets based on MT reference translations (Giménez and Màrquez, 2008; Carpuat and Wu, 2008), or manually constructed word sense disambiguation test beds that do not exactly match MT lexical choice (Carpuat and Wu, 2005). We will show how existing Cross-Lingual Word Sense Disambiguation tasks (Lefever and Hoste, 2010; Lefever and Hoste, 2013) can be directly seen as machine translation lexical choice (Section 2): their sense inventory is based on translations in a second language rather than arbitrary sense representations used in other WSD tasks (Carpuat and Wu, 2005); unlike in MT evaluation settings, human annotators can more easily provide a complete representation of all correct meanings of a word. Second, we show how using this task for evaluating the lexical choice performance of several phrase-based SMT systems (PBSMT) gives some insights into their strengths and weaknesses (Section 5).

2 Selecting a Word Sense Disambiguation Task to Evaluate MT Lexical Choice

Word Sense Disambiguation consists in determining the correct sense of a word in context. This challenging problem has been studied from a rich variety of persectives in Natural Language Processing (see Agirre and Edmonds (2006) for an overview.) The Senseval and SemEval series of evaluations (Edmonds and Cotton, 2001; Mihalcea and Edmonds, 2004; Agirre et al., 2007) have driven the standardization of methodology for evaluating WSD systems. Many shared tasks were organized over the years, providing evaluation settings that vary along several dimensions, including:

- target vocabulary: in *all word* tasks, systems are expected to tag all content words in running text (Palmer et al., 2001), while in *lexical sample* tasks, the evaluation considers a smaller predefined set of target words (Mihalcea et al., 2004; Lefever and Hoste, 2010).
- language: English is by far the most studied language, but the disambiguation of words in other languages such as Chinese (Jin et al., 2007) has been considered.
- sense inventory: many tasks use WordNet senses (Fellbaum, 1998), but other sense representations have been used, including alternate semantic databases such as HowNet (Dong, 1998), or lexicalizations in one or more languages (Chklovski et al., 2004).

The Cross-Lingual Word Sense Disambiguation (CLWSD) task introduced at a recent edition of SemEval (Lefever and Hoste, 2010) is an English lexical sample task that uses translations in other European languages as a sense inventory. As a result, it is particularly well suited to evaluating machine translation lexical choice.

2.1 Translations as Word Sense Representations

The CLWSD task is essentially the same task as MT lexical choice: given English target words in context, systems are asked to predict translations in other European languages. The gold standard consists of translations proposed by several bilingual humans, as can be seen in Table 1. MT system predictions can be compared to human annotations directly, without introducing additional sources of ambiguity and mismatches due to representation differences. This contrasts with our previous work on evaluating MT on a WSD task (Carpuat and Wu, 2005), which used text annotated with abstract sense categories from the HowNet knowledge base (Dong, 1998). In HowNet, each word is defined using a concept, constructed as a combination of basic units of meaning, called sememes. Words that share the same concept can be viewed as synonyms. Evaluating MT using a gold standard of HowNet categories requires to map translations from the MT output to the HowNet representation. Some categories are annotated with English translations, but additional effort is required in order to cover all translation candidates produced by the MT system.

2.2 Controlled Learning Conditions

Another advantage of the CLWSD task is that it provides controlled learning conditions (even though it is an unsupervised task with no annotated training data.) The gold labels for CLWSD are learned from parallel corpora. As a result MT lexical choice models can be estimated on the exact same data. Translations for English words in the lexical sample are extracted from a semi-automatic word alignment of

Target word	**ring**
English context	The twelve stars of the European flag are depicted on the outer **ring**.
Gold translations	anillo (3);círculo (2);corona (2);aro (1);
English context	The terrors which Mr Cash expresses about our future in the community have a familiar **ring** about them.
Gold translations	sonar (3);tinte (3);connotación(2);tono (1);
English context	The American containment **ring** around the Soviet bloc had been seriously breached only by the Soviet acquisition of military facilities in Cuba.
Gold translations	cerco (2);círculo (2);cordón (2);barrera (1);blindaje (1);limitación (1);

Table 1: Example of annotated CLWSD instances from the SemEval 2010 test set. For each gold Spanish translation, we are given the number of annotators who proposed it (out of 3 annotators.)

sentences from the Europarl parallel corpus (Koehn, 2005). These translations are then manually clustered into senses. When constructing the gold annotation, human annotators are given occurrences of target words in context. For each occurrence, they select a sense cluster and provide all translations from this cluster that are correct in this specific context. Since three annotators contribute, each test occurrence is therefore tagged with a set of translations in another language, along with a frequency which represents the number of annotators who selected it. A more detailed description of the annotation process can be found in (Lefever and Hoste, 2010).

Again, this contrasts with our previous work on evaluating MT on a HowNet-based Chinese WSD task, where Chinese sentences were manually annotated with HowNet senses which were completely unrelated to the parallel corpus used for training the SMT system. Using CLWSD as an evaluation of MT lexical choice solves this issue and provides controlled learning conditions.

2.3 CLWSD evaluates the semantic adequacy of MT lexical choice

A key challenge in MT evaluation lies in deciding whether the meaning of the translation is correct when it does not exactly match the reference translation. METEOR uses WordNet synonyms and learned paraphrases tables (Denkowski and Lavie, 2010). MEANT uses vector-space based lexical similarity scores (Lo et al., 2012). While these methods lead to higher correlations with human judgements on average, they are not ideal for a fine-grained evaluation of lexical choice: similarity scores are defined independently of context and might give credit to incorrect translations (Carpuat et al., 2012). In contrast, CLWSD solves this difficult problem by providing all correct translation candidates in context according to several human annotators. These multiple translations provide a more complete representation of the correct meaning of each occurrence of a word in context.

The CLWSD annotation procedure is designed to easily let human annotators provide many correct translation alternatives for a word. Producing many correct annotations for a complete sentence is a much more expensive undertaking: crowdsourcing can help alleviate the cost of obtaining a small number of reference translation (Zbib et al., 2012), but acquiring a complete representation of all possible translations of a source sentence is a much more complex task (Dreyer and Marcu, 2012). Machine translation evaluations typically use between one and four reference translations, which provide a very incomplete representation of the correct semantics of the input sentence in the output language. CLWSD provides a more complete representation through the multiple gold translations available.

2.4 Limitations

The main drawback of using CLWSD to evaluate lexical choice is that CLWSD is a lexical sample task, which only evaluates disambiguation of 20 English nouns. This arbitrary sample of words does not let us target words or phrases that might be specifically interesting for MT.

In addition, the data available through the shared task does not let us evaluate complete translations of the CLWSD test sentences, since full references translations are not available. Instead of using a WSD dataset for MT purposes, we could take the converse approach andautomatically construct a WSD test set based on MT evaluation corpora (Vickrey et al., 2005; Giménez and Màrquez, 2008; Carpuat and Wu, 2008; Carpuat et al., 2012). However, this approach suffers from noisy automatic alignments between source and reference, as well as from a limited representation of the correct meaning of words in context due to the limited number of reference translations.

Other SemEval tasks such as the Cross-Lingual Lexical Substitution Task (Mihalcea et al., 2010) would also provide an appropriate test bed. We focused on the CLWSD task, since it uses senses drawn from the Europarl parallel corpus, and therefore offers more constrained settings for comparison between systems. The lexical substitution task targets verbs and adjectives in addition to nouns, and would therefore be an interesting test case to consider in future work.

2.5 Official and MT-centric Evaluation Metrics

In order to make comparison with other systems possible, we follow the standard evaluation framework defined for the task and score the output of all our systems using four different metrics, computed using the scoring tool made available by the organizers.

The difference between system predictions and gold standard annotations are quantified using *precision* and *recall* scores[1] , defined as follows. Given a set T of test items and a set H of annotators, H_i is the set of translation proposed by all annotators h for instance $i \in T$. Each translation type res in H_i has an associated frequency $freq_{res}$, which represents the number of human annotators which selected res as one of their top 3 translations. Given a set of system answers A of items $i \in T$ such that the system provides at least one answer, $a_i : i \in A$ is is the set of answers from the system for instance i. For each i, the scorer computes the intersection of the system answers a_i and the gold standard H_i.

Systems propose as many answers as deemed necessary, but the scores are divided by the number of guesses in order not to favor systems that output many answers per instance.

$$\text{Precision} = \frac{1}{|A|} \sum_{a_i : i \in A} \frac{\sum_{res \in a_i} freq_{res}}{|a_i||H_i|}$$

$$\text{Recall} = \frac{1}{|T|} \sum_{a_i : i \in T} \frac{\sum_{res \in a_i} freq_{res}}{|a_i||H_i|}$$

We also report *Mode Precision* and *Mode Recall* scores: instead of comparing system answers to the full set of gold standard translations H_i for an instance $i \in T$, the Mode Precision and Recall scores only use a single gold translation, which is the translation chosen most frequently by the human annotators.

In addition, we compute the *1-gram precision* component of the BLEU score (Papineni et al., 2002), denoted as BLEU1 in the result tables[2]. In contrast with the official CLWSD evaluation scores described above, BLEU1 gives equal weight to all translation candidates, which can be seen as multiple references.

3 PBSMT system

We use a typical phrase-based SMT system trained for English-to-Spanish translation. Its application to the CLWSD task affects the selection of training data and its preprocessing, but the SMT model design and learning strategies are exactly the same as for conventional translation tasks.

3.1 Model

We use the NRC's PORTAGE phrase-based SMT system, which implements a standard phrasal beam-search decoder with cube pruning. Translation hypotheses are scored according to the following features:

- 4 phrase-table scores: phrasal translation probabilites with Kneser-Ney smoothing and Zens-Ney lexical smoothing in both translation directions (Chen et al., 2011)
- 6 hierarchical lexicalized reordering scores, which represent the orientation of the current phrase with respect to the previous block that could have been translated as a single phrase (Galley and Manning, 2008)

[1] In this paper, we focus on evaluating translation systems whose task is to produce a single complete translation for a given sentence. As a result, we only focus on the 1-best MT output and do not report the relaxed out-of-five evaluation setting also considered in the official SemEval task.

[2] even though it does not include the length penalty used in the BLEU score.

- a word penalty, which scores the length of the output sentence
- a word-displacement distortion penalty
- a Kneser-Ney smoothed 5-gram Spanish language model

Weights for these features are learned using a batch version of the MIRA algorithm(Cherry and Foster, 2012). Phrase pairs are extracted from IBM4 alignments obtained with GIZA++(Och and Ney, 2003). We learn phrase translation candidates for phrases of length 1 to 7.

Converting the PBSMT output for CLWSD requires a final straightforward mapping step. We use the phrasal alignment between SMT input and output to isolate the translation candidates for the CLWSD target word. When it maps to a multi-word phrase in the target language, we use the word within the phrase that has the highest translation IBM1 translation probability given the CLWSD target word of interest. Note that there is no need to perform any manual mapping between SMT output and sense inventories as in (Carpuat and Wu, 2005).

3.2 Data

The core training corpus is the exact same set of sentences from Europarl that were used to learn the sense inventory, in order to ensure that PBSMT knows the same translations as the human annotators who built the gold standard. There are about 900k sentence pairs, since only 1-to1 alignments that exist in all the languages considered in CLWSD were used (Lefever and Hoste, 2010).

We exploit additional corpora from the WMT2012 translation task, using the full Europarl corpus to train language models, and for one experiment the news-commentary parallel corpus (see Section 9.)

These parallel corpora are used to learn the translation, reordering and language models. The log-linear feature weights are learned on a development set of 3000 sentences sampled from the WMT2012 development test sets. They are selected based on their distance to the CLWSD trial and test sentences (Moore and Lewis, 2010).

We tokenize and lemmatize all English and Spanish text using the FreeLing tools (Padró and Stanilovsky, 2012). We use lemma representations to perform translation, since the CLWSD targets and translations are lemmatized.

4 WSD system

4.1 Model

We also train a dedicated WSD system for this task in order to perform a controlled comparison with the SMT system. Many WSD systems have been evaluated on the SemEval test bed used here, however, they differ in terms of resources used, training data and preprocessing pipelines. In order to control for these parameters, we build a WSD system trained on the exact same training corpus, preprocessing and word alignment as the SMT system described above.

We cast WSD as a generic ranking problem with linear models. Given a word in context x, translation candidates t are ranked according to the following model: $f(x,t) = \sum_i \lambda_i \phi_i(x,t)$, where $\phi_i(x,t)$ represent binary features that fire when specific clues are observed in a context x.

Context clues are based on standard feature templates in many supervised WSD approaches (Florian et al., 2002; van Gompel, 2010; Lefever et al., 2011):

- words in a window of 2 words around the disambiguation target.
- part-of-speech tags in a window of 2 words around the disambiguation target
- bag-of-word context: all nouns, verbs and adjectives in the context x

At training time, each example (x,t) is assigned a cost based on the translation observed in parallel corpora: $f(x,t) = 0$ if $t = t_{aligned}$, $f(x,t) = 1$ otherwise . Feature weights λ_i can be learned in many ways. We optimize logistic loss using stochastic gradient descent[3].

4.2 Data

The training instances for the supervised WSD system are built automatically by (1) extracting all occurrences of English target words in context, and (2) annotating them with their aligned Spanish lemma.

[3] we use the optimizer from http://hunch.net/~ vw v7.1.2

System	Prec.	Rec.	Mode Prec.	Mode Rec.	BLEU1
WSD	25.96	25.58	55.02	54.13	76.06
PBSMT	23.72	23.69	45.49	45.37	62.72
MFStest	21.35	21.35	44.50	44.50	65.50
MFStrain	19.14	19.14	42.00	42.00	59.70

Table 2: Main CLWSD results: PBSMT yields competitive results, but WSD outperforms PBSMT

System	Prec.	Rec.	Mode Prec.	Mode Rec.	BLEU1
PBSMT	23.72	23.69	45.49	45.37	62.72
max source phrase length l					
$l = 1$	24.44	24.36	44.50	44.38	65.43
$l = 3$	24.27	24.22	46.52	46.41	64.33
n-gram LM order					
$n = 3$	23.60	23.55	44.58	44.47	61.62
$n = 7$	23.58	23.53	46.06	45.94	62.22
$n = 2$	23.40	23.35	44.75	44.63	63.02
$n = 1$	22.92	22.87	43.00	42.89	58.62
+bilingual LM					
4-gram	23.89	23.84	45.49	45.37	62.62

Table 3: Impact of source and target context models on PBSMT performance

We obtain a total of 33139 training instances for all targets (an average of 1656 per target, with a minimum of 30 and a maximum of 5414). Note that this process does not require any manual annotation.

5 WSD systems can outperform PBSMT

Table 2 summarizes the main results. PBSMT outperforms the most frequent sense baseline by a wide margin, and interestingly also yields better results than many of the dedicated WSD systems that participated in the SemEval task. However, PBSMT performance does not match that of the most frequent sense oracle (which uses sense frequencies observed in the test set rather than training set). The WSD system trained on the same word-aligned parallel corpus as the PBSMT system achieves the best performance. It also obtains better results than all but the top system in the official results (Lefever and Hoste, 2010).

The results in Table 2 are quite different from those reported by Carpuat and Wu (2005) on a Chinese WSD task. The Chinese-English PBSMT system performed much worse than any of the dedicated WSD systems on that task. While our WSD system outperforms PBSMT on the CLWSD task too, the difference is not as large, and the PBSMT system is competitive when compared to the full set of systems that were evaluated on this task. This confirms that the CLWSD task represents a more fair benchmark for comparing PBSMT with WSD systems.

6 Impact of PBSMT Context Models

What is the impact of PBSMT context models on lexical choice accuracy? Table 3 provides an overview of experiments where we vary the context size available to the PBSMT system. The main PBSMT system in the top row uses the default settings presented in Section 3.

In the first set of experiments, we evaluate the impact of the source side context on CLWSD performance. Phrasal translations represent the core of PBSMT systems: they capture collocational context in the source language, and they are therefore are less ambiguous than single words (Koehn and Knight, 2003; Koehn et al., 2003). The default PBSMT learns translations for sources phrases of length ranging from 1 to 7 words.

Limiting the PBSMT system to translate shorter phrases (Rows $l = 1$ and $l = 3$ in Table 3) surprisingly improves CLWSD performance, even though it degrades BLEU score on WMT test sets. The source context captured by longer phrases therefore does not provide the right disambiguating information in this context.

In the second set of experiments, we evaluate the impact of the context size in the target language, by varying the size of the n-gram language model used. The default PBSMT system used a 5-gram language model. Reducing the n-gram order to 3, 2, 1 and increasing it to 7 both degrade performance. Shorter n-grams do not provide enough disambiguating context, while longer n-grams are more sparse and perhaps do not generalize well outside of the training corpus.

Finally, we report a last experiment which uses a bilingual language model to enrich the context representation in PBSMT (Niehues et al., 2011). This language model is estimated on word pairs formed

System	Prec.	Rec.	Mode Prec.	Mode Rec.	BLEU1
+ hier	23.72	23.69	45.49	45.37	62.72
+ lex	23.69	23.64	46.66	46.54	62.22
dist	23.42	23.37	45.43	45.30	62.22

Table 4: Impact of reordering models: lexicalized reodering does not hurt lexical choice only when hierarchical models are used

by target words augmented with their aligned source words. We use a 4-gram model, trained using Good-Turing discounting. This only results in small improvements (< 0.1) over the standard PBSMT system, and remains far below the performance of the dedicated WSD system.

These results show that source phrases are weak representations of context for the purpose of lexical choice. Target $n-gram$ context is more useful than source phrasal context, which can surprisingly harm lexical choice accuracy.

7 Impact of PBSMT Reordering Models

While the phrase-table is the core of PBSMT system, the reordering model used in our system is heavily lexicalized. In this section, we evaluate its impact on CLWSD performance. The standard PBSMT system uses a hierarchical lexicalized reordering model (Galley and Manning, 2008) in addition to the distance-based distortion limit. Unlike lexicalized reordering(Koehn et al., 2007), which models the orientation of a phrase with respect to the previous phrase, hierarchical reordering models define the orientation of a phrase with respect to the previous block that could have been translated as a single phrase.

In Table 4, we show that lexicalized reordering model benefit CLWSD performance, and that the hierarchical model performs slightly better than the non-hierarchical overall.

8 Impact of phrase translation selection

In this section, we consider the impact of various methods for selecting phrase translations on the lexical choice performance of PBSMT.

First, we investigate the impact of limiting the number of translation candidates considered for each source phrase in the phrase-table. The main PBSMT system uses $t = 50$ translation candidates per source phrase. Limiting that number to 20 and increasing it to 100 both have a very small impact on CLWSD.

System	Prec.	Rec.	Mode Prec.	Mode Rec.	BLEU1
PBSMT	23.72	23.69	45.49	45.37	62.72
Number t of translations per phrase					
$t = 20$	23.68	23.63	45.66	45.54	62.32
$t = 100$	23.65	23.60	45.65	45.53	62.52
Other phrase-table pruning methods					
stat sig	23.71	23.66	45.19	45.07	62.62

Table 5: Impact of translation candidate selection on PBSMT performance

Second, we prune the phrase-table using a statistical significance test to measure (Johnson et al., 2007). This pruning strategy aims to drastically decrease the size of the phrase-table without degrading translation performance by removing noisy phrase pairs.

9 Impact of training corpus

Since increasing the amount of training data is a reliable way to improve translation performance, we evaluate the impact of training the PBSMT system on more than the Europarl data used for controlled comparison with WSD. We increase the parallel training corpus with the WMT-12 News Commentary parallel data [4]. This yields an additional training set of roughly160k sentence pairs. We build linear mixture models to combine translation, reordering and language models learned on Europarl and News Commentary corpora (Foster and Kuhn, 2007). As can be seen in Table 6, this approach improves all CLWSD scores except for 1-gram precision. The decrease in 1-gram precision indicates that the addition of the news corpus introduces new translation candidates that differ from those used in the gold inventory. Interestingly, the additional data is not sufficient to match the performance of the WSD system learned on Europarl only (see Table 2). While additional data should be used when available, richer context features are valuable to make the most of existing data.

[4]http://www.statmt.org/wmt12/translation-task.html

System	Prec.	Rec.	Mode Prec.	Mode Rec.	BLEU1
Europarl	23.72	23.69	45.49	45.37	62.72
+ News	24.34	24.28	47.49	47.37	61.22

Table 6: Impact of training corpus on PBSMT performance: adding news parallel sentences helps Precision and Recall, but does not match WSD on the Europarl only.

10 Conclusion

We use a SemEval Cross-Lingual WSD task to evaluate the lexical choice performance of a typical phrase-based SMT system. Unlike conventional WSD task that rely on abstract sense inventories rather than translations, cross-lingual WSD provides a fair setting for comparing SMT with dedicated WSD systems. Unlike conventional evaluations of machine translation quality, the cross-lingual WSD task lets us isolate a specific aspect of translation quality and show how it is affected by different components of the phrase-based SMT system.

Unlike in previous evaluations on conventional WSD tasks (Carpuat and Wu, 2005), phrase-based SMT performance is on par with many dedicated WSD systems. However, the phrase-based SMT system does not perform as well as a WSD system trained on the exact same parallel data. Analysis shows that while many SMT components can potentially have an impact on SMT lexical choice, CLWSD accuracy is most affected by the length of source phrases and order of target n-gram language models. Using shorter source phrases actually improves lexical choice accuracy. The official results for the CLWSD task at SemEval 2013 evaluation provide further insights (Lefever and Hoste, 2013): our PBSMT system can achieve top precision as measured using the top prediction as in this paper, but does not perform as well as other submitted systems when taking into account the top 5 predictions (Carpuat, 2013). This suggests that local context models based on source phrases and target n-grams are much weaker representations of context than the simple templates used by WSD systems, and that even strong PBSMT systems can benefit from context models developed for WSD.

New learning algorithms (Chiang et al., 2009; Cherry and Foster, 2012, for instance) finally make it possible for PBSMT to reliably learn from many more features than the typical system used here. Evaluations such as the CLWSD task will provide useful tools for analyzing the impact of these features on lexical choice and inform feature design in increasingly large and complex systems.

References

E. Agirre and P.G. Edmonds. 2006. *Word Sense Disambiguation: Algorithms and Applications.* Text, Speech, and Language Technology Series. Springer Science+Business Media B.V.

Eneko Agirre, Lluís Màrquez, and Richard Wicentowski, editors. 2007. *Proceedings of SemEval-2007: 4th International Workshop on Semantic Evaluation*, Prague, July.

Satanjeev Banerjee and Alon Lavie. 2005. METEOR: An Automatic Metric for MT Evaluation with Improved Correlation with Human Judgement. In *Proceedings of Workshop on Intrinsic and Extrinsic Evaluation Measures for MT and/or Summarization at the 43th Annual Meeting of the Association of Computational Linguistics (ACL-2005)*, Ann Arbor, Michigan, June.

Alexandra Birch, Mile Osborne, and Phil Blunsom. 2010. Metrics for MT evaluation: Evaluating reordering. *Machine Translation*, 24:15–26.

Chris Callison-Burch, Philipp Koehn, Christof Monz, Kay Peterson, Mark Przybocki, and Omar F. Zaidan. 2010. Findings of the 2010 joint workshop on statistical machine translation and metrics for machine translation. In *Proceedings of the Joint Fifth Workshop on Statistical Machine Translation and MetricsMATR*, WMT '10, pages 17–53.

Marine Carpuat and Dekai Wu. 2005. Evaluating the Word Sense Disambiguation Performance of Statistical Machine Translation. In *Proceedings of the Second International Joint Conference on Natural Language Processing (IJCNLP)*, pages 122–127, Jeju Island, Republic of Korea.

Marine Carpuat and Dekai Wu. 2008. Evaluation of Context-Dependent Phrasal Translation Lexicons for Statistical Machine Translation. In *Proceedings of the sixth conference on Language Resouces and Evaluation (LREC 2008)*, Marrakech, May.

Marine Carpuat, Hal Daumé III, Alexander Fraser, Chris Quirk, Fabienne Braune, Ann Clifton, Ann Irvine, Jagadeesh Jagarlamudi, John Morgan, Majid Razmara, Aleš Tamchyna, Katharine Henry, and Rachel

Rudinger. 2012. Domain adaptation in machine translation: Final report. In *2012 Johns Hopkins Summer Workshop Final Report.*

Marine Carpuat. 2013. Nrc: A machine translation approach to cross-lingual word sense disambiguation (SemEval-2013 Task 10). In *Proceedings of SemEval.*

Boxing Chen, Roland Kuhn, George Foster, and Howard Johnson. 2011. Unpacking and transforming feature functions: New ways to smooth phrase tables. In *Proceedings of Machine Translation Summit.*

Boxing Chen, Roland Kuhn, and Samuel Larkin. 2012. Port: a precision-order-recall mt evaluation metric for tuning. In *Proceedings of the 50th Annual Meeting of the Association for Computational Linguistics*, pages 930–939.

Colin Cherry and George Foster. 2012. Batch tuning strategies for statistical machine translation. In *Proceedings of the 2012 Conference of the North American Chapter of the Association for Computational Linguistics: Human Language Technologies*, pages 427–436, Montréal, Canada, June.

David Chiang, Kevin Knight, and Wei Wang. 2009. 11,001 new features for statistical machine translation. In *NAACL-HLT 2009: Proceedings of the 2009 Annual Conference of the North American Chapter of the Association for Computational Linguistics*, pages 218–226, Boulder, Colorado.

Timothy Chklovski, Rada Mihalcea, Ted Pedersen, and Amruta Purandare. 2004. The Senseval-3 Multilingual English-Hindi lexical sample task. In *Proceedings of Senseval-3, Third International Workshop on Evaluating Word Sense Disambiguation Systems*, pages 5–8, Barcelona, Spain, July.

Michael Denkowski and Alon Lavie. 2010. METEOR-NEXT and the METEOR paraphrase tables: improved evaluation support for five target languages. In *Proceedings of the Joint Fifth Workshop on Statistical Machine Translation and MetricsMATR*, WMT '10, pages 339–342.

Zhendong Dong. 1998. Knowledge description: what, how and who? In *Proceedings of International Symposium on Electronic Dictionary*, Tokyo, Japan.

Markus Dreyer and Daniel Marcu. 2012. Hyter: Meaning-equivalent semantics for translation evaluation. In *Proceedings of the 2012 Conference of the North American Chapter of the Association for Computational Linguistics: Human Language Technologies*, pages 162–171, Montréal, Canada, June.

Philip Edmonds and Scott Cotton. 2001. Senseval-2: Overview. In *Proceedings of Senseval-2: Second International Workshop on Evaluating Word Snese Disambiguation Systems*, pages 1–5, Toulouse, France.

Christiane Fellbaum, editor. 1998. *WordNet: An Electronic Lexical Database.* MIT Press.

Radu Florian, Silviu Cucerzan, Charles Schafer, and David Yarowsky. 2002. Combining classifiers for word sense disambiguation. *Natural Language Engineering*, 8(4):327–241.

George Foster and Roland Kuhn. 2007. Mixture-model adaptation for SMT. In *Proceedings of the Second Workshop on Statistical Machine Translation*, pages 128–135, Prague, Czech Republic, June.

Michel Galley and Christopher D. Manning. 2008. A simple and effective hierarchical phrase reordering model. In *Proceedings of the Conference on Empirical Methods in Natural Language Processing*, EMNLP '08, pages 848–856.

Jesús Giménez and Lluís Márquez. 2007. Linguistic Features for Automatic Evaluation of Heterogenous MT Systems. In *Proceedings of the Second Workshop on Statistical Machine Translation*, pages 256–264, Prague

Jesús Giménez and Lluís Màrquez. 2008. Discriminative Phrase Selection for Statistical Machine Translation. *Learning Machine Translation. NIPS Workshop Series.*

Peng Jin, Yunfang Wu, and Shiwen Yu. 2007. Semeval-2007 task 05: Multilingual chinese-english lexical sample. In *Proceedings of the Fourth International Workshop on Semantic Evaluations (SemEval-2007)*, pages 19–23, Prague, Czech Republic, June.

Howard Johnson, Joel Martin, George Foster, and Roland Kuhn. 2007. Improving Translation Quality by Discarding Most of the Phrasetable. In *Proceedings of the 2007 Joint Conference on Empirical Methods in Natural Language Processing and Computational Natural Language Learning (EMNLP-CoNLL)*, pages 967–975.

Philipp Koehn and Kevin Knight. 2003. Feature-Rich Statistical Translation of Noun Phrases. In *Proceedings of 41st Annual Meeting of the Association for Computational Linguistics*, Sapporo, Japan, July.

Philipp Koehn, Franz Och, and Daniel Marcu. 2003. Statistical Phrase-based Translation. In *Proceedings of HLT/NAACL-2003*, Edmonton, Canada, May.

Philipp Koehn, Hieu Hoang, Alexandra Birch, Chris Callison-Burch, Marcello Federico, Nicola Bertoldi, Brooke Cowan, Wade Shen, Christine Moran, Richard Zens, Chris Dyer, Ondrej Bojar, Alexandra Constantin, and Evan Herbst. 2007. Moses: Open Source Toolkit for Statistical Machine Translation. In *Annual Meeting of the Association for Computational Linguistics (ACL), demonstration session*, Prague, Czech Republic, June.

Philipp Koehn. 2005. Europarl: A parallel corpus for statistical machine translation. In *Machine Translation Summit X*, Phuket, Thailand, September.

Els Lefever and Véronique Hoste. 2010. Semeval-2010 task 3: Cross-lingual word sense disambiguation. In *Proceedings of the 5th International Workshop on Semantic Evaluation*, pages 15–20, Uppsala, Sweden, July.

Els Lefever and Véronique Hoste. 2013. Semeval-2013 task 10: Cross-lingual word sense disambiguation. In *Proceedings of the 7th International Workshop on Semantic Evaluation (SemEval 2013)*, Atlanta, USA, May.

Els Lefever, Véronique Hoste, and Martine De Cock. 2011. Parasense or how to use parallel corpora for word sense disambiguation. In *Proceedings of the 49th Annual Meeting of the Association for Computational Linguistics: Human Language Technologies*, pages 317–322, Portland, Oregon, USA, June.

Chi-kiu Lo and Dekai Wu. 2011. Meant: an inexpensive, high-accuracy, semi-automatic metric for evaluating translation utility via semantic frames. In *Proceedings of the 49th Annual Meeting of the Association for Computational Linguistics: Human Language Technologies - Volume 1*, HLT '11, pages 220–229.

Chi-kiu Lo, Anand Karthik Tumuluru, and Dekai Wu. 2012. Fully automatic semantic MT evaluation. In *Proceedings of the Seventh Workshop on Statistical Machine Translation*, pages 243–252.

Rada Mihalcea and Phiip Edmonds, editors. 2004. *Proceedings of Senseval-3: Third international Workshop on the Evaluation of Systems for the Semantic Analysis of Text*, Barcelona, Spain.

Rada Mihalcea, Timothy Chklovski, and Adam Killgarriff. 2004. The Senseval-3 English lexical sample task. In *Proceedings of Senseval-3, Third International Workshop on Evaluating Word Sense Disambiguation Systems*, pages 25–28, Barcelona, Spain, July.

Rada Mihalcea, Ravi Sinha, and Diana McCarthy. 2010. SemEval-2010 Task 2: Cross-Lingual Lexical Substitution. In *Proceedings of the 5th International Workshop on Semantic Evaluation*, pages 9–14, Uppsala, Sweden, July.

Robert C. Moore and William Lewis. 2010. Intelligent selection of language model training data. In *Proceedings of the ACL 2010 Conference Short Papers*, ACLShort '10, pages 220–224, Stroudsburg, PA, USA.

Jan Niehues, Teresa Herrmann, Stephan Vogel, and Alex Waibel. 2011. Wider context by using bilingual language models in machine translation. In *Proceedings of the Sixth Workshop on Statistical Machine Translation*, WMT '11, pages 198–206, Stroudsburg, PA, USA.

Franz Josef Och and Hermann Ney. 2003. A Systematic Comparison of Various Statistical Alignment Models. *Computational Linguistics*, 29(1):19–52.

Lluís Padró and Evgeny Stanilovsky. 2012. FreeLing 3.0: Towards wider multilinguality. In *Proceedings of the Language Resources and Evaluation Conference (LREC 2012)*, Istanbul, Turkey, May.

Martha Palmer, Christiane Fellbaum, Scott Cotton, Lauren Delfs, and Hao Trang Dang. 2001. English tasks: All-words and verb lexical sample. In *Proceedings of Senseval-2, Second International Workshop on Evaluating Word Sense Disambiguation Systems*, pages 21–24, Toulouse, France, July. SIGLEX, Association for Computational Linguistic.

Kishore Papineni, Salim Roukos, Todd Ward, and Wei-Jing Zhu. 2002. BLEU: a method for automatic evaluation of machine translation. In *Proceedings of the 40th Annual Meeting of the Association for Computational Linguistics*, Philadelphia, PA, July.

Maarten van Gompel. 2010. Uvt-wsd1: A cross-lingual word sense disambiguation system. In *Proceedings of the 5th International Workshop on Semantic Evaluation*, pages 238–241, Uppsala, Sweden, July.

David Vickrey, Luke Biewald, Marc Teyssier, and Daphne Koller. 2005. Word-Sense Disambiguation for Machine Translation. In *Joint Human Language Technology conference and Conference on Empirical Methods in Natural Language Processing (HLT/EMNLP 2005)*, Vancouver.

David Vilar, Jia Xu, Luis Fernando D'Haro, and Hermann Ney. 2006. Error Analysis of Machine Translation Output. In *Proceedings of the 5th International Conference on Language Resources and Evaluation (LREC'06)*, pages 697–702, Genoa, Italy, May.

Rabih Zbib, Erika Malchiodi, Jacob Devlin, David Stallard, Spyros Matsoukas, Richard Schwartz, John Makhoul, Omar F. Zaidan, and Chris Callison-Burch. 2012. Machine translation of arabic dialects. In *Proceedings of the 2012 Conference of the North American Chapter of the Association for Computational Linguistics: Human Language Technologies*, NAACL HLT '12, pages 49–59.

Taste of Two Different Flavours: Which Manipuri Script Works Better for English-Manipuri Language Pair SMT Systems?

Thoudam Doren Singh
Centre for Development of Advanced Computing (CDAC), Mumbai
Gulmohor Cross Road No 9, Juhu
Mumbai-400049, INDIA
thoudam.doren@gmail.com

Abstract

The statistical machine translation (SMT) system heavily depends on the sentence aligned parallel corpus and the target language model. This paper points out some of the core issues on switching a language script and its repercussion in the phrase based statistical machine translation system development. The present task reports on the outcome of English-Manipuri language pair phrase based SMT task on two aspects – a) Manipuri using Bengali script, b) Manipuri using transliterated Meetei Mayek script. Two independent views on Bengali script based SMT and transliterated Meitei Mayek based SMT systems of the training data and language models are presented and compared. The impact of various language models is commendable in such scenario. The BLEU and NIST score shows that Bengali script based phrase based SMT (PBSMT) outperforms over the Meetei Mayek based English to Manipuri SMT system. However, subjective evaluation shows slight variation against the automatic scores.

1 Introduction

The present finding is due to some issue of sociolinguistics phenomenon called digraphia - a case of Manipuri language (a resource constrained Indian languages spoken mainly in the state of Manipur) using two different scripts namely Bengali script[1] and Meetei Mayek[2]. Meetei Mayek (MM) is the original script which was used until the 18th century to represent Manipuri text. Its earliest use is dated between the 11th and 12th centuries CE[3]. Manipuri language is recognized by the Indian Union and has been included in the list of 8th scheduled languages by the 71st amendment of the constitution in 1992. In the recent times, the Bengali script is getting replaced by Meetei Mayek at schools, government departments and other administrative activities. It may be noted that Manipuri is the only Tibeto-Burman language which has its own script. Digraphia has implications in language technology as well despite the issues of language planning, language policy and language ideology. There are several examples of languages written in one script that was replaced later by another script. Some of the examples are Romanian which originally used Cyrillic then changed to Latin; Turkish and Swahili began with the Arabic then Latin, and many languages of former Soviet Central Asia, which abandoned the Cyrillic script after the dissolution of the USSR. The present study is a typical case where the natural language processing of an Indian language is affected in case of switching script.

Manipuri is a monosyllabic, morphologically rich and highly agglutinative in nature. Tone is very prominent. So, a special treatment of these tonal words is absolutely necessary. Manipuri language has 6 vowels and their tone counterparts and 6 diphthongs and their tone counterparts. Thus, a

[1] http://unicode.org/charts/PDF/U0980.pdf

[2] http://unicode.org/charts/PDF/UABC0.pdf
[3] http://en.wikipedia.org/wiki/Meitei_language

Manipuri learner should know its tone system and the corresponding word meaning.

Natural language processing tasks for Manipuri language is at the initial phase. We use a small parallel corpus and a sizable monolingual corpus collected from Manipuri news to develop English-Manipuri statistical machine translation system. The Manipuri news texts are in Bengali script. So, we carry out transliteration from Bengali script to Meetei Mayek as discussed in section 3. Typically, transliteration is carried out between two different languages –one as a source and the other as a target. But, in our case, in order to kick start the MT system development, Bengali script (in which most of the digital Manipuri text are available) to Meetei Mayek transliteration is carried out using different models. The performance of the rule based transliteration is improved by integrating the conjunct and syllable handling module in the present rule based task along with transliteration unit (TU). However, due to the tonal characteristic of this language, there is loss of accents for the tonal words when getting translated from Bengali script. In other words, there is essence of intonation in Manipuri text; the differentiation between Bengali characters such as ি (i) and ী (ee) or ু (u) and ূ (oo) cannot be made using Meetei Mayek. This increases the lexical ambiguity on the transliterated Manipuri words in Meetei Mayek script.

2 Related Work

Several SMT systems between English and morphologically rich languages are reported. (Toutonova et al., 2007) reported the improvement of an SMT by applying word form prediction models from a stem using extensive morphological and syntactic information from source and target languages. Contributions using factored phrase based model and a probabilistic tree transfer model at deep syntactic layer are made by (Bojar and Hajič, 2008) of English-to-Czech SMT system. (Yeniterzi and Oflazer, 2010) reported syntax-to-morphology mapping in factored phrase-based Statistical Machine Translation (Koehn and Hoang, 2007) from English to Turkish relying on syntactic analysis on the source side (English) and then encodes a wide variety of local and non-local syntactic structures as complex structural tags which appear as additional factors in the training data. On the target side (Turkish), they only perform morphological analysis and disambiguation but treat the complete complex morphological tag as a factor, instead of separating morphemes. (Bojar et al., 2012) pointed out several pitfalls when designing factored model translation setup. All the above systems have been developed using one script for each language at the source as well as target.

Manipuri is a relatively free word order where the grammatical role of content words is largely determined by their case markers and not just by their positions in the sentence. Machine Translation systems of Manipuri and English is reported by (Singh and Bandyopadhyay, 2010b) on development of English-Manipuri SMT system using morpho-syntactic and semantic information where the target case markers are generated based on the suffixes and semantic relations of the source sentence. The above mentioned system is developed using Bengali script based Manipuri text. SMT systems between English and morphologically rich highly agglutinative language suffer badly if the adequate training and language resource is not available. Not only this, it is important to note that the linguistic representation of the text has implications on several NLP aspects not only in machine translations systems. This is our first attempt to build and compare English-Manipuri language pair SMT systems using two different scripts of Manipuri.

3 Transliterated Parallel Corpora

The English-Manipuri parallel corpora and Manipuri monolingual corpus collected from the news website www.thesangaiexpress.com are based on Bengali script. The Bengali script has 52 consonants and 12 vowels. The modern-day Meetei Mayek script is made up of a core repertoire of 27 letters, alongside letters and symbols for final consonants, dependent vowel signs, punctuation, and digits. Meetei Mayek is a Brahmic script with consonants bearing the inherent vowel and vowel matras modifying it. However, unlike most other Brahmi-derived scripts, Meetei Mayek employs explicit final consonants which contain no final vowels. The use of the killer (which refers to its function of *killing* the inherent vowel of a consonant letter) is optional in spelling; for example, while ꯗꯔ may be read *dara* or *dra*, ꯗ꯭ꯔ must be read *dra*. Syllable initial combinations for vowels can occur in modern usage to represent diphthongs. The Meetei Mayek has 27 letters (Iyek Ipee), 8 dependent vowel signs (Cheitap Iyek), 8 final consonants (Lonsum Iyek), 10 digits (Cheising Iyek) and 3 punctuation (Cheikhei, Lum Iyek and Apun Iyek).

Bengali Script	**Meetei Mayek**
ষ, স, শ, ছ	ꯁ (Sam)
ন, ণ	ꯅ (Na)
ট, ত	ꯇ (Til)
থ, ঠ	ꯊ (Thou)
য়, য	ꯌ (Yang)
দ, ড	ꯗ (Dil)
ঢ, ধ	ꯙ (Dhou)
উ, ঊ	ꯎ (Un)
ই, ঈ	ꯏ (Ee)
র, ড়, ঢ়	ꯔ (Rai)
ি, ী	ꯤ (Inap)
ু, ূ	ꯨ (Unap)

Table 1 – Many-to-One mapping table

There is no possibility of direct one-to-one mapping for the 27 Meetei Mayek letter (Iyek Ipee) to Bengali script as given by table 1, over and above some of Bengali scripts which does not have a corresponding direct mapping to Meetei Mayek such as (ঋ, ক্ষ, ঃ, ঞ, ঁ etc.) which has resulted in the loss of target representation. The syllable based Bengali script to Meetei Mayek transliteration system outperforms the other known transliteration systems in news domain between the two scripts in terms of precision and recall (Singh, 2012). The overall conjunct representation is many-to-many characters in nature for the bilingual transliteration task of Bengali script and Meetei Mayek. Some of the example words using the conjuncts are given as:

প্রেসনা ←→ ꯄ꯭ꯔꯦꯁꯅ (*press-na*)

ডিষ্ট্রিককি ←→ ꯗꯤꯁ꯭ꯇ꯭ꯔꯤꯛꯀꯤ (*district-ki*)

সেক্রেটরিয়েত্তা ←→ ꯁꯦꯀ꯭ꯔꯦꯇꯔꯤꯌꯦꯠꯇ (*secretariate-ta*)

পেট্রোল ←→ ꯄꯦꯇ꯭ꯔꯣꯜ (*petrol*)

And the Bengali script conjuncts and its constituents along with the Meetei Mayek notation for the above examples are as given below:

প্রে (pre) → প + ্র + ে → ꯄ꯭ꯔꯦ

ষ্ট্রি (stri) → ষ + ট + ্র + ি → ꯁ꯭ꯇ꯭ꯔꯤ

ক্রে (cre) → ক + র + ে → ꯀ꯭ꯔꯦ

ট্রো (tro) → ট + র + ো → ꯇ꯭ꯔꯣ

A sample transliterated parallel corpus between English and Manipuri is given in the table 2. These transliterations are based on the syllable based model.

English	On the part of the election department, IFCD have been intimidated for taking up necessary measures.
Manipuri in Bengali Script	ইলেক্সন ডিপার্টমেন্টকি মায়কৈদগী আইএফসিডিদা দরকার লৈবা থবক পায়খত্নবা খঙহনখ্রে .
Manipuri in Meetei Mayek	ꯏꯂꯦꯛꯁꯟ ꯗꯤꯄꯥꯔ꯭ꯇꯃꯦꯟ꯭ꯇꯀꯤ ꯃꯥꯌꯀꯩꯗꯒꯤ ꯑꯥꯏꯑꯦꯐꯁꯤꯗꯤꯗꯥ ꯗꯔꯀꯥꯔ ꯂꯩꯕꯥ ꯊꯕꯛ ꯄꯥꯌꯈꯠꯅꯕꯥ ꯈꯉꯍꯟꯈ꯭ꯔꯦ ॥
Gloss	*election departmentki maykeidagee IFCDda darkar leiba thabak paykhatnaba khanghankhre .*
English	In case of rising the water level of Nambul river, the gate is shut down and the engines are operated to pump out the water.
Manipuri in Bengali Script	করিগুম্বা নম্বুল তুরেলগী ঈশিং ইমায় ৱাংখত্লক্লবদি গেট অসি থিংলগা ঈশিং অসি ইঞ্জিননা ওইনা চিংথোক্লগা লাকপনি হায়রি .
Manipuri in Meetei Mayek	ꯀꯔꯤꯒꯨꯝꯕ ꯅꯝꯕꯨꯜ ꯇꯨꯔꯦꯂꯒꯤ ꯏꯁꯤꯡ ꯏꯃꯥꯌ ꯋꯥꯡꯈꯠꯂꯛꯂꯕꯗꯤ ꯒꯦꯠ ꯑꯁꯤ ꯊꯤꯡꯂꯒꯥ ꯏꯁꯤꯡ ꯑꯁꯤ ꯏꯟꯖꯤꯅꯅꯥ ꯑꯣꯏꯅꯥ ꯆꯤꯡꯊꯣꯛꯂꯒꯥ ꯂꯥꯛꯄꯅꯤ ꯍꯥꯌꯔꯤ ॥
Gloss	*karigumba nambul turelgi eesing eemay waangkhatlaklabadi gate asi thinglaga eesing asi enginena oyna chingthoklaga laakpani hayri.*
English	The department has a gate at Samushang meant for draining out the flood water of Lamphelpat.
Manipuri in Bengali Script	শামুশঙদা ডিপার্টমেন্ট অসিগী গেট অমা লম্ফেলপাৎকি ঈশিং চিংথোক্লবা থম্মী .
Manipuri in Meetei Mayek	ꯁꯃꯨꯁꯡꯗꯥ ꯗꯤꯄꯥꯔ꯭ꯇꯃꯦꯟ꯭ꯇ ꯑꯁꯤꯒꯤ ꯒꯦꯠ ꯑꯃꯥ ꯂꯝꯐꯦꯜꯄꯥꯠꯀꯤ ꯏꯁꯤꯡ ꯆꯤꯡꯊꯣꯛꯅꯕꯥ ꯊꯝꯃꯤ ॥
Gloss	*samusangda department asigee gate ama lamphelpatki easing chingthoknaba thammee.*

Table 2. Transliterated texts of English – Manipuri Parallel Corpora and the corresponding Gloss

4 Building SMT for English-Manipuri

The important resources of building SMT are the training and language modeling data. We use a small amount of parallel corpora for training and a sizable amount of monolingual Manipuri and English news corpora. So, we have two aspects of developing English-Manipuri language pair SMT systems by using the two different scripts for Manipuri. The moot question is which script will perform better. At the moment, we are developing only the baseline systems. So, the downstream tools are not taken into account which would have affected by way of the performance of the script specific tools other than the transliteration system performance used in the task. In the SMT development process, apart from transliteration accuracy error, the change in script to represent Manipuri text has made the task of NLP related activities a difference in the way how it was carried out with Bengali script towards improving the factored based modes in future as well. Lexical ambiguity is very common in this language mostly due to tonal characteristics. This has resulted towards the requirement of a word sense disambiguation module more than before. This is because of a set of difference in the representation using Meitei Mayek. As part of this ongoing experiment, we augment the training data with 4600 manually prepared variants of verbs and nouns phrases for improving the overall accuracy and help solving a bit of data sparsity problem of the SMT system along with an additional lexicon of 10000 entries between English and Manipuri to handle bits of data sparsity and sense disambiguation during the training process. The English-Manipuri parallel corpus developed by (Singh and Bandyopadhyay, 2010a) is used in the experiment. Moses[4] toolkit (Koehn, 2007) is used for training with GIZA++[5] and decoding. Minimum error rate training (Och, 2003) for tuning are carried out using the development data for two scripts. Table 3 gives the corpus statistics of the English-Manipuri SMT system development.

4.1 Lexical Ambiguity

Manipuri is, by large, a tonal language. The lexical ambiguity is very prominent even with Bengali script based text representation. The degree of ambiguity worsens due to the convergence as shown by the figure 1 and many to one mapping shown in the table 1. So, the Bengali script to Meetei Mayek transliteration has resulted to the lost of several words meaning at the transliterated output. Many aspects of translation can be best explained at a morphological, syntactic or semantic level. This implies that the phrase table and target language model are very much affected by using Meetei Mayek based text and hence the output of the SMT system. Thus, lexical ambiguity is one major reason on why the transliterated Meetei Mayek script based PBSMT suffers comparatively. Three examples of lexical ambiguity are given below:

(a)
মি (*mi*) → *spider* → ꯃꯤ (*mi*) meaning either *spider* or *man*

মী (*mee*) → *man* → ꯃꯤ (*mi*) meaning either *spider* or *man*

(b)
শূবা (*sooba*) → to work → ꯁꯨꯕ (*suba*) meaning either *to work* or *to hit*

শুবা (*suba*) → to hit → ꯁꯨꯕ (*suba*) meaning either *to work* or *to hit*

(c)
সিনবা (*sinba*) / শিনবা (*shinba*) → substitution → ꯁꯤꯟꯕ (*sinba*)

শীনবা (*sheenba*) → arrangement → ꯁꯤꯟꯕ (*sinba*)

শীনবা (*sheenba*) → sour taste → ꯁꯤꯟꯕ (*sinba*)

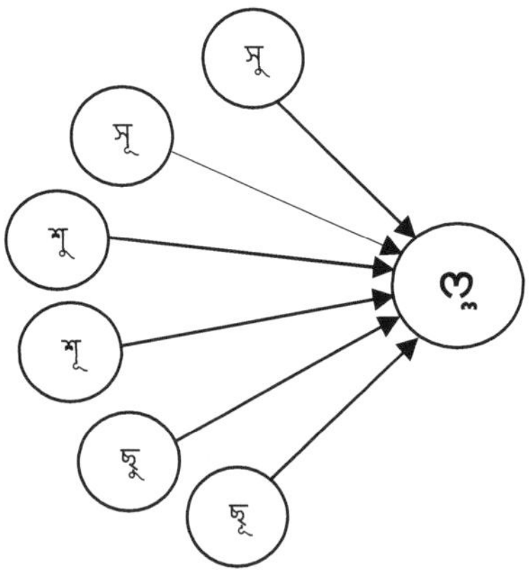

Figure 1. An example of convergence of TU (সু -su, সূ-soo etc.) from Bengali Script to Meitei Mayek

[4] http://www.statmt.org/moses/
[5] http://www.fjoch.com/GIZA++.html

The lexical ambiguity that arises are twofold, i) one after transliteration into Meetei Mayek as given by examples (a) and (b), ii) one before the transliteration as given by the example (c) for which the ambiguity is doubled after the transliteration. Thus, the scripts are functioning as a representation language for lexical ambiguity like the semantic phrase sense disambiguation model for SMT (Carpuat and Wu, 2007).

4.2 Language Modeling

The impact of the different language models is clearly seen in our experiment mostly by way of lexical variation and convergence characteristics as shown in Figure 1. Four different language models are developed: a) language model (LM1) on Bengali script based Manipuri text, b) language model (LM2) on transliterated Manipuri Meetei Mayek text, there is change in the language model parameter such as perplexity which affects the overall translation decoding process, c) language model (LM3) based on language model (LM1) with transliteration to Meitei Mayek on Manipuri text from Bengali Script texts, and d) language model (LM4) based on language model (LM2) with transliteration to Bengali script on Manipuri text from Meetei Mayek text. SRILM (Stolcke, 2002) is used to build trigram model with modified Kneser-Ney smoothing (Stanley and Joshua, 1998) and interpolated with lower order estimates which works best for Manipuri language using 2.3 million words of 180,000 Manipuri news sentences. There are variations in the language model parameters while switching the scripts.

The log probability and perplexity of the sentence (considering the first sentence from Table 2) using Bengali script, "ইলেক্সন ডিপার্টমেন্টকি মায়কৈদগী আইএফসিডিদা দরকার লৈবা থবক পায়থস্নবা থঙহনখ্রে ।" are given as:

logprob= -22.873 ppl= 193.774 ppl1= 347.888

while the parameters for the same sentence using Meetei Mayek, i.e.,

"[illegible] ॥" are given as:

logprob= -26.7555 ppl= 473.752 ppl1= 939.364

It is also observed that some of the n-grams entries on one language model are not available in the other language model. For example,

-2.708879 মদুদা চেন্নবনি -0.3211589

is a bigram found in Bengali script based language model but not found in the Meetei Mayek based language model. Similarly,

-6.077539 [illegible] -0.06379553

is a bigram found in the Meetei Mayek based language model but not available in Bengali script based language model. Above all, for the same n-gram in the language models, the log(P(W)) and log(backoff-weight) are found to be different. Two bigram examples are given below:

-1.972813 মদুদা খোল্পকপা -0.09325081
-6.077539 [illegible] -0.06379553

and,

-1.759148 মদুদা খোরকপা -0.3929711
-6.077539 [illegible] -0.06379552

4.3 Evaluation

The systems are developed using the following corpus statistics.

	# of Sentences	# of Words
Training	10000	231254
Development	5000	121201
Testing	500	12204

Table 3. Corpus Statistics

The evaluations of SMT systems are done using automatic scoring and subjective evaluation.

4.4 Automatic Scoring

We carry out the comparisons of automatic evaluation metrics scores for the SMT systems. The various models developed are evaluated using BLEU (Papineni et al, 2002) and NIST (Doddington, 2002) automatic scoring techniques. A high NIST score means a better translation by measuring the precision of n-gram.

	BLEU Score	NIST Score
Meetei Mayek based Baseline using LM2 language model	11.05	3.57
Meetei Mayek based Baseline with LM3 language model	11.81	3.33
Bengali Script based Baseline using LM1 language model	15.02	4.01
Bengali Script based Baseline using LM4 language model	14.51	3.82

Table 4 . Automatics Scores of English to Manipuri SMT system

BLEU metric gives the precision of n-gram with respect to the reference translation but with a brevity penalty.

	BLEU Score	NIST Score
Bengali Script based Baseline	12.12	4.27
Meetei Mayek based Baseline using	13.74	4.31

Table 5. Automatics Scores of Manipuri to English SMT system

4.5 Subjective Evaluation

The subjective evaluation is carried out by two bilingual judges. The inter-annotator agreement is 0.3 of scale 1. The adequacy and fluency used in the subjective evaluation scales are given by the Table 6 and Table 7.

Level	Interpretation
4	Full meaning is conveyed
3	Most of the meaning is conveyed
2	Poor meaning is conveyed
1	No meaning is conveyed

Table 6. Adequacy Scale

Level	Interpretation
4	Flawless with no grammatical error
3	Good output with minor errors
2	Disfluent ungrammatical with correct phrase
1	Incomprehensible

Table 7. Fluency Scale

The scores of adequacy and fluency on 100 test sentences based on the length are given at Table 8 and Table 9 based on the adequacy and fluency scales give by Table 6 and Table 7.

	Sentence length	Fluency	Adequacy
Baseline using Bengali Script	<=15 words	3.13	3.16
	>15 words	2.21	2.47
Baseline using Meetei Mayek	<=15 words	3.58	3.47
	>15 words	2.47	2.63

Table 8. Scores of Adequacy and Fluency of English to Manipuri SMT system

	Sentence length	Fluency	Adequacy
Baseline using Bengali Script	<=15 words	2.39	2.42
	>15 words	2.01	2.14
Baseline using Meetei Mayek	<=15 words	2.61	2.65
	>15 words	2.10	1.94

Table 9. Scores of Adequacy and Fluency of Manipuri to English SMT system

5 Sample Translation Outputs

The following tables show the various translation outputs of English-Manipuri as well as Manipuri-English PBSMT systems using Bengali script and Meetei Mayek scripts.

English	On the part of the election department, IFCD have been intimidated for taking up necessary measures.
Manipuri Reference Translation (Bengali Script)	ইলেক্সন ডিপার্টমেন্টকি মায়কৈদগী আইএফসিডিদা দরকার লৈবা থবক পায়খত্নবা খঙহনখ্রে .
Gloss	*election departmentki maykeidagee IFCDda darkar leiba thabak paykhatnaba khanghankhre .*
Baseline Translation output (Bengali Script)	ইলেক্সন ডিপার্টমেন্টকি মায়কৈদগী আইএফসিডিদা দরকার লৈবা থবক পায়খত্নবা খঙহনখ্রে.

Table 10. English to Manipuri SMT system output using Bengali Script

English	On the part of the election department, IFCD have been intimidated for taking up necessary measures.
Manipuri reference Translation (Meetei Mayek)	[illegible]
Gloss	*election departmentki maykeidagee IFCDda darkar leiba thabak paykhatnaba khanghankhre .*
Baseline Translation output	[illegible]

Table 11: English to Manipuri SMT system output using Meetei Mayek

Input Manipuri sentence	ইলেক্সন ডিপার্টমেন্টকি মায়কৈদগী আইএফসিডিদা দরকার লৈবা থবক পায়খত্নবা খঙহনখ্রে .
Gloss	*election departmentki maykeidagee IFCDda darkar leiba thabak paykhatnaba khanghankhre .*
Reference English translation	On the part of the election department, IFCD have been intimidated for taking up necessary measures.
Baseline Translation output	the election department notified IFCD to take up necessary steps

Table 12: Manipuri to English translation output using Bengali script:

Input Manipuri sentence	[illegible]
Gloss	*election departmentki maykeidagee IFCDda darkar leiba thabak paykhatnaba khanghankhre .*
Reference English translation	On the part of the election department, IFCD have been intimidated for taking up necessary measures.
Baseline Translation output	the election department intimidated IFCD to take up necessary steps

Table 13: Manipuri to English translation output using Meetei Mayek:

The English to Manipuri SMT system output using Bengali Script suffers fluency and adequacy scores as given by table 8 compared to English to Manipuri SMT system output using Meetei Mayek script. In the case of Manipuri to English SMT system, the Meetei Mayek based SMT system outperforms the Bengali script based SMT in terms of both fluency and adequacy as given by table 9 as well as automatic scores as given by table 5.

6 Conclusion and Discussion

The detailed study of grapheme-to-phoneme indicates missing tone for several words using present Meetei Mayek script. The training process based on the Bengali script training data is found to have higher vocabulary coverage all across since the representation is done with a finer glyph as compared to Meetei Mayek so is the higher automatic scores in case of English-to-Manipuri PBSMT system. But, considering the subjective evaluation scores, the Meetei Mayek based SMT systems outperforms the Bengali script based English-to-Manipuri SMT systems as against the automatic scores. In the case of Manipuri-to-English PBSMT systems, both the automatic score and subjective evaluation scores using Meetei Mayek outperforms the Bengali script based systems. Statistical significant test is performed to judge if a change in score that comes from a change in the system with script switching reflects a change in overall translation quality. The systems show statistically significant result as measured by bootstrap resampling method (Koehn, 2004) on BLEU score. In future, the experiments can be repeated with special treatment of individual morphemes in bits and pieces on a decent size of parallel corpora. More notably, SMT decoders may have the feature of handling two or more scripts of the same language in the future SMT systems for languages like Manipuri.

Acknowledgments

I, sincerely, thank Dr. Zia Saquib, Executive Director, CDAC (Mumbai), Prof. Sivaji Bandyopadhyay, Jadavpur University, Kolkata and the anonymous reviewers for their support and valuable comments.

References

Andreas Stolcke. 2002. *SRILM – an extensible language modeling toolkit.* In Proceedings of the International Conference on Spoken Language Processing.

Franz J. Och. 2003. *Minimum error rate training in Statistical Machine Translation*, Proceedings of ACL.

George Doddington. 2002. *Automatic evaluation of Machine Translation quality using n-gram co-occurrence statistics.* In Proceedings of HLT 2002, San Diego, CA.

Kishore Papineni, Salim Roukos, Todd Ward and Wei-Jing Zhu. 2002. *BLEU: a method for automatic evaluation of machine translation.* In Proceedings of 40th ACL, Philadelphia, PA.

Kristina Toutanova, Hisami Suzuki and Achim Ruopp. 2008. *Applying Morphology Generation Models to Machine Translation*, In Proc. 46th Annual Meeting of the Association for Computational Linguistics.

Marine Carpuat and Dekai Wu. 2007. *How Phrase Sense Disambiguation outperforms Word Sense Disambiguation for Statistical Machine,* 11th International Conference on Theoretical and Methodological Issues in Machine Translation (TMI 2007). pages 43-52, Skövde, Sweden, September 2007.

Ondřej Bojar and Jan Hajič. 2008. *Phrase-Based and Deep Syntactic English-to-Czech Statistical Machine Translation*, Proceedings of the Third Workshop on Statistical Machine Translation, pages 143–146, Columbus, Ohio, USA.

Ondřej Bojar, Bushra Jawaid and Amir Kamran. 2012. *Probes in a Taxonomy of Factored Phrase-Based Models*, Proceedings of the 7th Workshop on Statistical Machine Translation of Association for Computational Linguistics, pages 253–260, Montréal, Canada.

Philipp Koehn. 2004. *Statistical significance tests for machine translation evaluation.* In EMNLP-2004: Proceedings of the 2004 Conference on Empirical Methods in Natural Language Processing, 25-26 July 2004, pages 388-395, Barcelona, Spain.

Philipp Koehn, Hieu Hoang, Alexandra Birch, Chris Callison-Burch, Marcello Federico, Nicola Bertoldi, Brooke Cowan, Wade Shen, Christine Moran, Richard Zens, Chris Dyer, Ondřej Bojar, Alexandra Constantin and Evan Herbst. 2007. *Moses: Open Source Toolkit for Statistical Machine Translation*, Annual Meeting of the Association for Computational Linguistics (ACL), demonstration session, Prague, Czech Republic.

Reyyan Yeniterzi and Kemal Oflazer. 2010. *Syntax-to-Morphology Mapping in Factored Phrase-Based Statistical Machine Translation from English to Turkish*, In proceeding of the 48th Annual Meeting of the Association of Computational Linguistics, Pages 454-464, Uppsala, Sweden.

Stanley F. Chen and Joshua Goodman. 1998. *An empirical study of smoothing techniques for language modeling*. Technical Report TR-10-98, Harvard University Center for Research in Computing Technology.

Thoudam Doren Singh and Sivaji Bandyopadhyay. 2010a. *Semi Automatic Parallel Corpora Extraction from Comparable News Corpora*, In the International Journal of POLIBITS, Issue 41 (January – June 2010), ISSN 1870-9044, pages 11-17.

Thoudam Doren Singh and Sivaji Bandyopadhyay. 2010b. *Manipuri-English Bidirectional Statistical MachineTranslation Systems using Morphology and Dependency Relations*, Proceedings of SSST-4, Fourth Workshop on Syntax and Structure in Statistical Translation, pages 83–91, COLING 2010, Beijing, August 2010.

Thoudam Doren Singh. 2012. *Bidirectional Bengali Script and Meetei Mayek Transliteration of Web Based Manipuri News Corpus*, In the Proceedings of the 3rd Workshop on South and Southeast Asian Natural Language Processing (SANLP) of COLING 2012, IIT Bombay, Mumbai, India, pages 181-189, 8th December, 2012.

Hierarchical Alignment Decomposition Labels for Hiero Grammar Rules

Gideon Maillette de Buy Wenniger
Institute for Logic,
Language and Computation
University of Amsterdam
Science Park 904, 1098 XH Amsterdam
The Netherlands
`gemdbw AT gmail.com`

Khalil Sima'an
Institute for Logic,
Language and Computation
University of Amsterdam
Science Park 904, 1098 XH Amsterdam
The Netherlands
`k.simaan AT uva.nl`

Abstract

Selecting a set of nonterminals for the synchronous CFGs underlying the hierarchical phrase-based models is usually done on the basis of a monolingual resource (like a syntactic parser). However, a standard bilingual resource like word alignments is itself rich with reordering patterns that, if clustered somehow, might provide labels of different (possibly complementary) nature to monolingual labels. In this paper we explore a first version of this idea based on a hierarchical decomposition of word alignments into recursive tree representations. We identify five clusters of alignment patterns in which the children of a node in a decomposition tree are found and employ these five as nonterminal labels for the Hiero productions. Although this is our first non-optimized instantiation of the idea, our experiments show competitive performance with the Hiero baseline, exemplifying certain merits of this novel approach.

1 Introduction

The Hiero model (Chiang, 2007; Chiang, 2005) formulates phrase-based translation in terms of a synchronous context-free grammar (SCFG) limited to the inversion transduction grammar (ITG) (Wu, 1997) family. While the original Hiero approach works with a single nonterminal label (X) (besides the start nonterminal S), more recent work is dedicated to devising methods for extracting more elaborate labels for the phrase-pairs and their abstractions into SCFG productions, e.g., (Zollmann and Venugopal, 2006; Li et al., 2012; Almaghout et al., 2011). All labeling approaches exploit monolingual parsers of some kind, e.g., syntactic, semantic or sense-oriented. The rationale behind monolingual labeling is often to make the probability distributions over alternative synchronous derivations of the Hiero model more sensitive to linguistically justified monolingual phrase context. For example, syntactic target-language labels in many approaches are aimed at improved target language modeling (fluency, cf. Hassan et al. (2007); Zollmann and Venugopal (2006)), whereas source-language labels provide suitable context for reordering (see Mylonakis and Sima'an (2011)). It is usually believed that the monolingual labels tend to stand for clusters of phrase pairs that are expected to be inter-substitutable, either syntactically or semantically (see Marton et al. (2012) for an illuminating discussion).

While we believe that monolingual labeling strategies are sound, in this paper we explore the complementary idea that the nonterminal labels could also signify *bilingual properties of the phrase pair*, particularly its characteristic *word alignment patterns*. Intuitively, an SCFG with nonterminal labels standing for alignment patterns should put more preference on synchronous derivations that mimic the word alignment patterns found in the training corpus, and thus, possibly allow for better reordering. It is important to stress the fact that these word alignment patterns are complementary to the monolingual linguistic patterns and it is conceivable that the two can be combined effectively, but this remains beyond the scope of this article.

The question addressed in this paper is how to select word alignment patterns and cluster them into bilingual nonterminal labels? In this paper we explore a first instantiation of this idea starting out from the following simplifying assumptions:

- The labels come from the word alignments only,
- The labels are coarse-grained, pre-defined clusters and not optimized for performance,
- The labels extend the binary set of ITG operators (monotone and inverted) into five such labels in order to cover non-binarizable alignment patterns.

Our labels are based on our own tree decompositions of word alignments (Sima'an and Maillette de Buy Wenniger, 2011), akin to Normalized Decomposition Trees (NDTs) (Zhang et al., 2008). In this first attempt we explore a set of five nonterminal labels that characterize alignment patterns found directly under nodes in the NDT projected for every word alignment in the parallel corpus during training. There is a range of work that exploits the monotone and inverted orientations of binary ITG within hierarchical phrase-based models, either as feature functions of lexicalized Hiero productions (Chiang, 2007; Zollmann and Venugopal, 2006), or as labels on non-lexicalized ITG productions, e.g., (Mylonakis and Sima'an, 2011). As far as we are aware, this is the first attempt at exploring a larger set of such word alignment derived labels in hierarchical SMT. Therefore, we expect that there are many variants that could improve substantially on our strong set of assumptions.

2 Hierarchical SMT models

Hierarchical SMT usually works with *weighted* instantiations of Synchronous Context-Free Grammars (SCFGs) (Aho and Ullman, 1969). SCFGs are defined over a finite set of nonterminals (start included), a finite set of terminals and a finite set of synchronous productions. A synchronous production in an SCFG consists of two context-free productions (source and target) containing the same number of nonterminals on the right-hand side, with a bijective (1-to-1 and onto) function between the source and target nonterminals. Like the standard Hiero model (Chiang, 2007), we constrain our work to SCFGs which involve at most two nonterminals in every lexicalized production.

Given an SCFG G, a source sentence $\mathbf{s}$ is translated into a target sentence $\mathbf{t}$ by synchronous derivations $\mathbf{d}$, each is a finite sequence of well-formed substitutions of synchronous productions from G, see (Chiang, 2006). Standardly, for complexity reasons, most models used make the assumption that the probability $P(\mathbf{t} \mid \mathbf{s})$ can be optimized through as single best derivation as follows:

$$\arg\max_{\mathbf{t}} P(\mathbf{t} \mid \mathbf{s}) = \arg\max_{\mathbf{t}} \sum_{\mathbf{d} \in G} P(\mathbf{t}, \mathbf{d} \mid \mathbf{s}) \quad (1)$$

$$\approx \arg\max_{\mathbf{d} \in G} P(\mathbf{t}, \mathbf{d} \mid \mathbf{s}) \quad (2)$$

This approximation can be notoriously problematic for labelled Hiero models because the labels tend to lead to many more derivations than in the original model, thereby aggravating the effects of this assumption. This problem is relevant for our work and approaches to deal with it are Minimum Bayes-Risk decoding (Kumar and Byrne, 2004; Tromble et al., 2008), Variational Decoding (Li et al., 2009) and soft labeling (Venugopal et al., 2009; Marton et al., 2012; Chiang, 2010).

Given a derivation $\mathbf{d}$, most existing phrase-based models approximate the derivation probability through a linear interpolation of a finite set of feature functions ($\Phi(\mathbf{d})$) of the derivation $\mathbf{d}$, mostly working with local feature functions ϕ_i of individual productions, the target side yield string t of $\mathbf{d}$ (target language model features) and other heuristic features discussed in the experimental section:

$$\arg\max_{\mathbf{d} \in G} P(\mathbf{t}, \mathbf{d} \mid \mathbf{s}) \approx \arg\max_{\mathbf{d} \in G} \sum_{i=1}^{|\Phi(\mathbf{d})|} \lambda_i \times \phi_i \quad (3)$$

Where λ_i is the weight of feature ϕ_i optimized over a held-out parallel corpus by some direct error-minimization procedure like MERT (Och, 2003).

3 Baseline: Hiero Grammars (single label)

Hiero Grammars (Chiang, 2005; Chiang, 2007) are a particular form of SCFGs that generalize phrase-based translation models to hierarchical phrase-based Translation models. They allow only up to two (pairs of) nonterminals on the right-hand-side of rules. Hierarchical rules are formed from fully lexicalized base rules (i.e. phrase pairs) by replacing a sub-span of the phrase pair that corresponds itself to a valid phrase pair with variable X called "gap". Two gaps may be maximally introduced in this way[1], labeled as $X_{\boxed{1}}$ and $X_{\boxed{2}}$ respectively for distinction. The types of permissible Hiero rules are:

$$X \rightarrow \langle \alpha,\ \gamma \rangle \tag{4a}$$

$$X \rightarrow \langle \alpha\ X_{\boxed{1}}\beta,\ \delta\ X_{\boxed{1}}\zeta \rangle \tag{4b}$$

$$X \rightarrow \langle \alpha\ X_{\boxed{1}}\beta\ X_{\boxed{2}}\gamma\ ,\ \delta\ X_{\boxed{1}}\ \zeta\ X_{\boxed{2}}\eta\ \rangle \tag{4c}$$

$$X \rightarrow \langle \alpha\ X_{\boxed{1}}\beta\ X_{\boxed{2}}\gamma\ ,\ \delta\ X_{\boxed{2}}\ \zeta\ X_{\boxed{1}}\eta\ \rangle \tag{4d}$$

Here $\alpha, \beta, \gamma, \delta, \zeta, \eta$ are terminal sequences, possibly empty. Equation 4a corresponds to a normal phrase pair, 4b to a rule with one gap and 4c and 4d to the monotone- and inverting rules respectively.

An important extra constraint used in the original Hiero model is that rules must have at least one pair of aligned words, so that translation decisions are always based on some lexical evidence. Furthermore the sum of terminals and nonterminals on the source side may not be greater than five, and nonterminals are not allowed to be adjacent on the source side.

4 Alignment Labeled Grammars

Labeling the Hiero grammar productions makes rules with gaps more restricted about what broad categories of rules are allowed to substitute for the gaps. In the best case this prevents overgeneralization, and makes the translation distributions more accurate. In the worst case, however, it can also lead to too restrictive rules, as well as sparse translation distributions. Despite these inherent risks, a number of approaches based on syntactically inspired labels has succeeded to improve the state of the art by using monolingual labels, e.g., (Zollmann and Venugopal, 2006; Zollmann, 2011; Almaghout et al., 2011; Chiang, 2010; Li et al., 2012).

Unlabeled Hiero derivations can be seen as recursive compositions of phrase pairs. A single translation may be generated by different derivations (see equation 1), each standing for a choice of composition rules over a choice of a segmentation of the source-target sentence pair into a bag of phrase pairs. However, a synchronous derivation also induces an alignment between the different segments that it composes together. Our goal here is to label the Hiero rules in order to exploit aspects of the alignment that a synchronous derivation induces.

We exploit the idea that phrase pairs can be efficiently grouped into maximally decomposed trees (normalized decomposition trees – NDTs) (Zhang et al., 2008). In an NDT every phrase pair is recursively decomposed at every level into the *minimum number* of its phrase constituents, so that the resulting structure is maximal in that it contains the largest number of nodes. In Figure 1 left we show an example alignment and in Figure 1 right its associated NDT. The NDT shows pairs of source and target spans of (sub-) phrase pairs, governed at different levels of the tree by their parent node. In our example the root node splits into three phrase pairs, but these three phrase pairs together do not manage to cover the entire phrase pair of the parent because of the discontinuous translation structure ⟨owe, sind ... schuldig⟩. Consequently, a partially lexicalized structure with three children corresponding to phrase pairs and lexical items covering the words left by these phrase pairs is required.

During grammar extraction we determine an Alignment Label for every left-hand-side and gap of every rule we extract. This is done by looking at the NDT that decomposes their corresponding phrase pairs, and determining the complexity of the relation with their direct children in this tree. Complexity cases are ordered by preference, where the more simple label corresponding to the choice of maximal decomposition is preferred. We distinguish the following five cases, ordered by increasing complexity:

1. *Monotonic*: If the alignment can be split into two monotonically ordered parts.
2. *Inverted*: If the alignment can be split into two inverted parts.
3. *Permutation*: If the alignment can be factored as a permutation of more than 3 parts.[2]
4. *Complex*: If the alignment cannot be factored as a permutation of parts, but the phrase does contain at least one smaller phrase pair (i.e., it is composite).
5. *Atomic*: If the alignment does not allow the existence of smaller (child) phrase pairs.

[1]The motivation for this restriction to two gaps is mainly a practical computational one, as it can be shown that translation complexity grows exponentially with the number of gaps.

[2]Permutations of just 3 parts never occur in a NDT, as they can always be further decomposed as a sequence of two binary nodes.

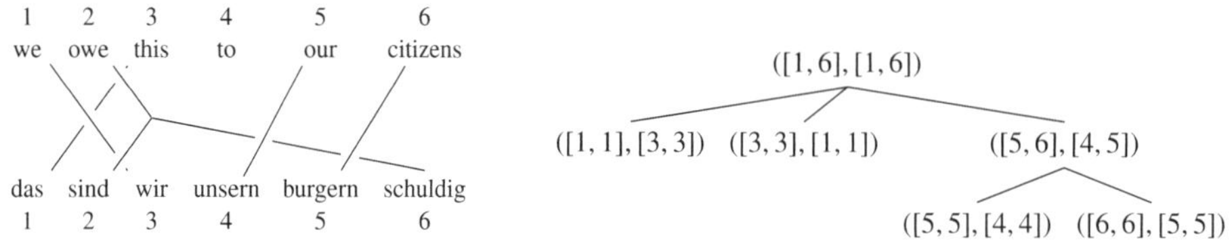

Figure 1: Example of complex word alignment, taken from Europarl data English-German (left) and its associated Normalized Decomposition Tree (Zhang et al., 2008) (right).

We show examples of each of these cases in Figure 2. Furthermore, in Figure 3 we show an example of an alignment labeled Hiero rule based on one of these alignment examples.

Our kind of labels has a completely different flavor from monolingual labels in that they cannot be seen as identifying linguistically meaningful clusters of phrase pairs. These labels are mere latent bilingual clusters and the translation model must marginalize over them (equation 1) or use Minimum Bayes-Risk decoding.

4.1 Features : Relations over labels

In this section we describe the features we use in our experiments. To be unambiguous we first need to introduce some terminology. Let r be a translation rule. We use $\hat{p}$ to denote probabilities estimated using simple relative frequency estimation from the word aligned sentence pairs of the training corpus. Then $src(r)$ is the source side of the rule, including the source side of the left-hand-side label. Similarly $tgt(r)$ is the target side of the rule, including the target side of the left-hand-side label. Furthermore $un(src(r))$ is the source side without any nonterminal labels, and analogous for $un(tgt(r))$.

4.1.1 Basic Features

We use the following phrase probability features:

- $\hat{p}(tgt(r)|src(r))$: Phrase probability target side given source side
- $\hat{p}(src(r)|tgt(r))$: Phrase probability source side given target side

We reinforce those by the following phrase probability smoothing features:

- $\hat{p}(tgt(r)|un(src(r)))$
- $\hat{p}(un(src(r))|tgt(r))$
- $\hat{p}(un(tgt(r))|src(r))$
- $\hat{p}(src(r)|un(tgt(r)))$
- $\hat{p}(un(tgt(r))|un(src(r)))$
- $\hat{p}(un(src(r))|un(tgt(r)))$

We also add the following features:

- $\hat{p}_w(tgt(r)|src(r))$, $\hat{p}_w(src(r)|tgt(r))$: Lexical weights based on terminal symbols as for phrase-based and hierarchical phrase-based MT.
- $\hat{p}(r|lhs(r))$: Generative probability of a rule given its left-hand-side label

We use the following set of basic binary features, with 1 values by default, and a value $exp(1)$ if the corresponding condition holds:

- $\varphi_{Glue}(r)$: $exp(1)$ if rule is a glue rule
- $\varphi_{lex}(r)$: $exp(1)$ if rule has only terminals on right-hand side
- $\varphi_{abs}(r)$: $exp(1)$ if rule has only nonterminals on right-hand side
- $\varphi_{st\_w\_tt}(r)$: $exp(1)$ if rule has terminals on the source side but not on the target side
- $\varphi_{tt\_w\_st}(r)$: $exp(1)$ if rule has terminals on the target side but not on the source side
- $\varphi_{mono}(r)$: $exp(1)$ if rule has no inverted pair of nonterminals

Furthermore we use the :

- $\varphi_{ra}(r)$: Phrase penalty, $exp(1)$ for all rules.
- $exp(\varphi_{wp}(r))$: Word penalty, exponent of the number of terminals on the target side
- $\varphi_{rare}(r)$: $exp(\frac{1}{\#(\sum_{r' \in C} \delta_{rr'})})$: Rarity penalty, with $\#(\sum_{r' \in C} \delta_{rr'})$ being the count of rule r in the corpus.

4.1.2 Binary Reordering Features

Besides the basic features we want to use extra sets of binary features that are specially designed to directly learn the desirability of certain broad classes of reordering patterns, beyond the way this is already implicitly learned for particular lexicalized rules by the introduction of reordering labels.[3] These features can be seen as generalizations of the most simple feature that penalizes/rewards mono-

[3]We did some initial experiments with such features in Joshua, but haven't managed yet to get them working in Moses with MBR. Since these experiments are inconclusive without MBR we leave them out here.

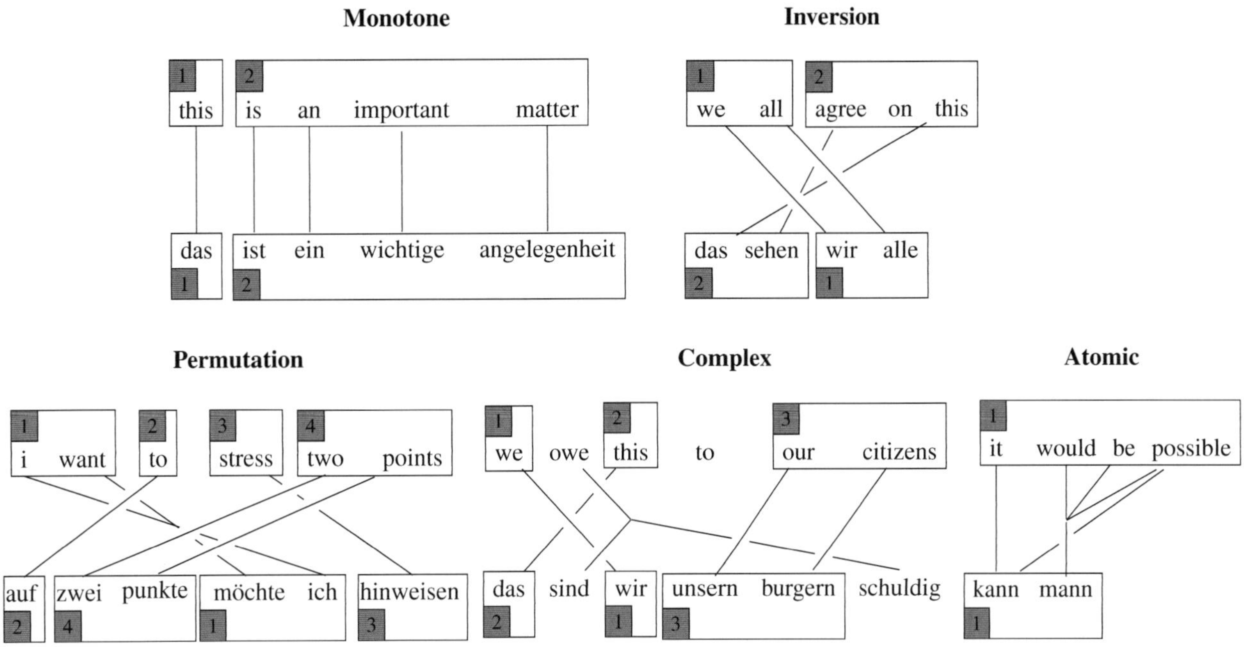

Figure 2: Different types of Alignment Labels

tone order $\varphi_{mono}(r)$ from our basic feature set. The new features we want to introduce "fire" for a specific combination of reordering labels on the left hand side and one or both gaps, plus optionally the information whether the rule itself invert its gaps and whether or not it is abstract.

5 Experiments

We evaluate our method on one language pair using German as source and English as target. The data is derived from parliament proceedings sourced from the Europarl corpus (Koehn, 2005), with WMT-07 development and test data. We used a maximum sentence length of 40 for filtering. We employ either 200K or (approximately) 1000K sentence pairs for training, 1K for development and 2K for testing (single reference per source sentence). Both the baseline and our method decode with a 3-gram language model smoothed with modified Knesser-Ney discounting (Chen and Goodman, 1998), trained on the target side of the full original training set (approximately 1000K sentences).

We compare against state-of-the-art hierarchical translation (Chiang, 2005) baselines, based on the Joshua (Ganitkevitch et al., 2012) and Moses (Hoang et al., 2007) translation systems with default decoding settings. We use our own grammar extractor for the generation of all grammars, including the baseline Hiero grammars. This enables us to use the same features (as far as applicable given the grammar formalism) and assure true comparability of the grammars under comparison.

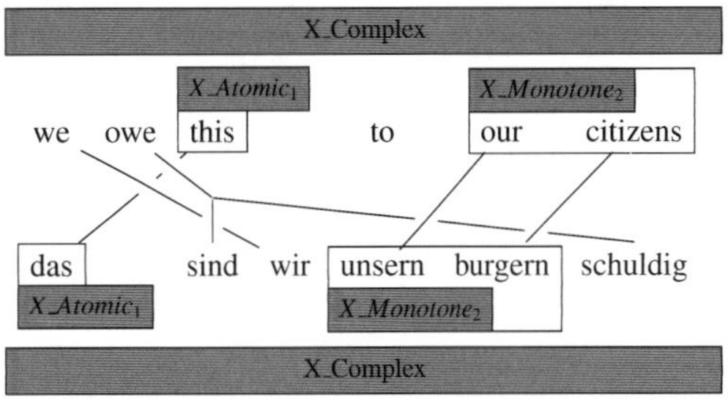

Figure 3: Example of a labeled Hiero rule
$X\_Complex \rightarrow$ ⟨we owe $X\_Atomic_{\boxed{1}}$ to $X\_Monotone_{\boxed{2}}$, $X\_Atomic_{\boxed{1}}$ sind wir $X\_Monotone_{\boxed{2}}$ schuldig ⟩
extracted from the *Complex* example in Figure 2 by replacing the phrase pairs ⟨this, das⟩ and ⟨our citizens , unsern burgern⟩ with (labeled) variables.

5.1 Training and Decoding Details

In this section we discuss the choices and settings we used in our experiments. Our initial experiments

[4] We later discovered we needed to add the flag "–return-best-dev" in Moses to actually get the weights from the best development run, our initial experiments had not used this. This explains the somewhat unfortunate drop in performance in our Analysis Experiments.

Decoding Type	System Name	**200K**
Lattice MBR	Hiero	26.44
	Hiero-RL	**26.72**
Viterbi	Hiero	26.23
	Hiero-RL-PPL	26.16

Table 1: Initial Results. Lowercase BLEU results for German-English trained on 200K sentence pairs.[4]
Top rows display results for our experiments using Moses (Hoang et al., 2007) with Lattice Minimum Bayes-Risk Decoding[5] (Tromble et al., 2008) in combination with Batch Mira (Cherry and Foster, 2012) for tuning. Below are results for experiments with Joshua (Ganitkevitch et al., 2012) using Viterbi decoding (i.e. no MBR) and PRO (Hopkins and May, 2011) for tuning.

were done on Joshua (Ganitkevitch et al., 2012), using the Viterbi best derivation. The second set of experiments was done on Moses (Hoang et al., 2007) using Lattice Minimum Bayes-Risk Decoding[5] (Tromble et al., 2008) to sum over derivations.

5.1.1 General Settings

To train our system we use the following settings. We use the standard Hiero grammar extraction constraints (Chiang, 2007) but for our reordering labeled grammars we use them with some modifications. In particular, while for basic Hiero only phrase pairs with source spans up to 10 are allowed, and abstract rules are forbidden, we allow extraction of fully abstract rules, without length constraints. Furthermore we allow their application without length constraints during decoding. Following common practice, we use simple relative frequency estimation to estimate the phrase probabilities, lexical probabilities and generative rule probability respectively.[6]

[5]After submission we were told by Moses support that in fact neither normal Minimum Bayes-Risk (MBR) nor Lattice MBR are operational in Moses Chart.

[6]Personal correspondence with Andreas Zollmann further reinforced the authors appreciation of the importance of this feature introduced in (Zollmann and Venugopal, 2006; Zollmann, 2011). Strangely enough this feature seems to be unavailable in the standard Moses (Hoang et al., 2007) and Joshua (Ganitkevitch et al., 2012) grammar extractors, that also implement SAMT grammar extraction

5.1.2 Specific choices and settings Joshua Viterbi experiments

Based on experiments reported in (Mylonakis and Sima'an, 2011; Mylonakis, 2012) we opted to not label the (fully lexicalized) phrase pairs, but instead label them with a generic *PhrasePair* label and use a set of switch rules from all other labels to the *PhrasePair* label to enable transition between Hiero rules and phrase pairs.

We train our systems using PRO (Hopkins and May, 2011) implemented in Joshua by Ganitkevitch et al. (2012). We use the standard tuning, where all features are treated as dense features.We allow up to 30 tuning iterations. We further follow the PRO settings introduced in (Ganitkevitch et al., 2012) but use 0.5 for the coefficient Ψ that interpolates the weights learned at the current with those from the previous iteration. We use the final learned weights for decoding with the log-linear model and report Lowercase BLEU scores for the tuned test set.

5.1.3 Specific choices and settings Moses Lattice MBR experiments

As mentioned before we use Moses (Hoang et al., 2007) for our second experiment, in combination with Lattice Minimum Bayes-Risk Decoding[5] (Tromble et al., 2008). Furthermore we use Batch Mira (Cherry and Foster, 2012) for tuning with maximum 10 tuning iterations of the 200K training set, and 30 for the 1000K training set.[7]

For our Moses experiments we mainly worked with a uniform labeling policy, labeling phrase pairs in the same way with alignment labels as normal rules. This is motivated by the fact that since we are using Minimum Bayes-Risk decoding, the risks of sparsity from labeling are much reduced. And labeling everything does have the advantage that reorder-

[7]We are mostly interested in the relative performance of our system in comparison to the baseline for the same settings. Nevertheless, it might be that the labeled systems, which have more smoothing features, are relatively suffering more from too little tuning iterations than the baseline which does not have these extra features and thus may be easier to tune. This was one of the reasons to increase the number of tuning iterations from 10 to 30 in our later experiments on 1000K. Usage of Minimum Bayes-Risk decoding or not is crucial as we have explained before in section 1. The main reason we opted for Batch Mira over PRO is that it is more commonly used in Moses systems, and in any case at least superior to MERT (Och, 2003) in most cases.

ing information can be fully propagated in derivations starting from the lowest (phrase) level. We also ran experiments with the generic phrase pair labeling, since there were reasons to believe this could decrease sparsity and potentially lead to better results.[8]

5.2 Initial Results

We report Lowercase BLEU scores for experiments with and without Lattice Minimum Bayes-Risk (MBR) decoding (Tromble et al., 2008). Table 1 bottom shows the results of our first experiments with Joshua, using the Viterbi derivation and no MBR decoding to sum over derivations. We display scores for the Hiero baseline (Hiero) and the (partially) alignment labeled system (Hiero-AL-PPL) which uses alignment labels for Hiero rules and PhrasePair to label all phrase pairs. Scores are around 26.25 BLEU for both systems, with only marginal differences. In summary our labeled systems are at best comparable to the Hiero baseline.

Table 1 top shows the results of our second experiments with Moses and Lattice MBR[5]. Here our (fully) alignment labeled system (Hiero-AL) achieves a score of 26.72 BLEU, in comparison to 26.44 BLEU for the Hiero baseline (Hiero). A small improvement of 0.28 BLEU point.

5.3 Advanced experiments

We now report Lowercase BLEU scores for more detailed analysis experiments with and without Lattice Minimum Bayes-Risk[5] (MBR) decoding, where we varied other training and decoding parameters in the Moses environment. Particularly, in this set of experiments we choose the *best tuning parameter settings* over 30 Batch Mira iterations (as opposed to the weights returned by default – used in the previous experiments). We also explore varieties in tuning with a decoder that works with Viterbi/MBR, and final testing with Viterbi/MBR.

In Table 2, the top rows show the results of our experiments using MBR decoding. We display scores for the Hiero baseline (Hiero) and the fully/partially alignment labeled systems Hiero-AL and Hiero-AL-PPL. In the preceding set of experiments MBR decoding clearly showed improved performance over Viterbi, particularly for our labelled system.

Decoding Type	System Name	**200K**	**1000K**
Lattice MBR	Hiero	27.19	28.39
	Hiero-AL	26.61	28.32
	Hiero-AL-PPL	26.89	28.41
Viterbi	Hiero	26.80	**28.57**
	Hiero-AL	———	28.36

Table 2: Analysis Results. Lowercase BLEU results for German-English trained on 200K and 1000K sentence pairs using Moses (Hoang et al., 2007) in combination with Batch Mira (Cherry and Foster, 2012) for tuning. Top rows display results for our experiments with Lattice Minimum Bayes-Risk Decoding[5] (Tromble et al., 2008). Below are results for experiments using Viterbi decoding (i.e. no MBR) for tuning. Results on 200K were run with 10 tuning iterations, results on 1000K with 30 tuning iterations.

On the small training set of 200K we observe that the Hiero baseline achieves 27.19 BLEU and thus beats the labeled systems Hiero-AL with 26.61 BLEU and 26.89 BLEU by a good margin. On the bigger dataset of 1000K and with more tuning iterations (3), all systems perform better. When using Lattice MBR Hiero achieving 28.39 BLEU, Hiero-AL 28.32 BLEU and finally Hiero-AL-PPL achieves 28.41. These are insignificant differences in performance between the labelled and unlabeled systems.

Table 1 bottom also shows the results of our second set of experiments with *Viterbi decoding*. Here, the baseline Hiero system for 200K training set achieves a score of 26.80 BLEU on the small training set. We also conducted another set of experiments on the larger training set of 1000K, this time with Viterbi decoding. The Hiero baseline with Viterbi scores 28.57 BLEU while Hiero-AL scores 28.36 BLEU under the same conditions.

It is puzzling that Hiero Viterbi (for 1000k) performs better than the same system with MBR decoding systems. But after submission we were told by Moses support that neither normal MBR nor Lattice MBR are operational in Moses Chart. This means that in fact the effect of MBR on our labels remains still undecided, and more work is still needed in this direction. The small decrease in performance for the

[8]We discovered that the Moses chart decoder does not allow fully abstract unary rules in the current implementation, which makes direct usage of unary (switch) rules not possible. Switch rules and other unaries can still be emulated though, by adapting the grammar, using multiple copies of rules with different labels. This blows up the grammar a bit, but at least works in practice.

labelled system relative to Hiero (in Viterbi) is possibly the result of the labelled system being more brittle and harder to tune than the Hiero system. This hypothesis needs further exploration.

While a whole set of experimental questions remains open, we think that based on this preliminary but nevertheless considerable set of experiments, it seems that our labels do not always improve performance compared with the Hiero baseline. It is possible that these labels, under a more advanced implementation via soft constraints (as opposed to hard labeling), could provide the empirical evidence to our theoretical choices. A further concern regarding the labels is that our current choice (5 labels) is heuristic and not optimized for the training data. It remains to be seen in the future if proper learning of these labels as latent variables optimized for the training data or the use of soft constraints can shed more light on the use of alignment labels in hierarchical SMT.

5.4 Analysis

While we did not have time to do a deep comparative analysis of the properties of the grammars, a few things can be said based on the results. First of all we have seen that alignment labels do not always improve over the Hiero baseline. In earlier experiments we observed some improvement when the labelled grammar was used in combination with Minimum Bayes-Risk Decoding but not without it. In later experiments with different tuning settings (Mira), the improvements evaporated and in fact, the Viterbi Hiero baseline turned out, surprisingly, the best of all systems.

Our use of MBR is theoretically justified by the importance of aggregating over the derivations of the output translations when labeling Hiero variables: statistically speaking, if the labels split the occurrences of the phrase pairs, they will lead to multiple derivations per Hiero derivation with fractions of the scores. This is in line with earlier work on the effect of spurious ambiguity, e.g. Variational Decoding (Li et al., 2009). Yet, in the case of our model, there is also a conceptual explanation for the need to aggregate over different derivations of the same sentence pair. The decomposition of a word alignment into hierarchical decomposition trees has a interesting property: the simpler (less reordering) a word alignment, the more (binary) decomposition trees – and in our model derivations – it will have. Hence, aggregating over the derivations is a way to gather evidence for the complexity of alignment patterns that our model can fit in between a given source-target sentence pair. However, in the current experimental setting, where final tuning with Mira is crucial, and where the use of MBR within Moses is still not standard, we cannot reap full benefit of our theoretical analysis concerning the fit of MBR for our models' alignment labels.

6 Conclusion

We presented a novel method for labeling Hiero variables with nonterminals derived from the hierarchical patterns found in recursive decompositions of word alignments into tree representations. Our experiments based on a first instantiation of this idea with a fixed set of labels, not optimized to the training data, show promising performance. Our early experiments suggested that these labels have merit, whereas later experiments with more varied training and decoder settings showed these results to be unstable.

Empirical results aside, our approach opens up a whole new line of research to improve the state of the art of hierarchical SMT by learning these latent alignment labels directly from standard word alignments without special use of syntactic or other parsers. The fact that such labels are in principle complementary with monolingual information is an exciting perspective which we might explore in future work.

Acknowledgements

This work is supported by The Netherlands Organization for Scientific Research (NWO) under grant nr. 612.066.929. This work was sponsored by the BIG Grid project for the use of the computing and storage facilities, with financial support from the Netherlands Organization of Scientific Research (NWO) under grant BG-087-12. The authors would like to thank the people from the Joshua team at John Hopkins University, in particular Yuan Cao, Jonathan Weese, Matt Post and Juri Ganitkevitch, for their helpful replies to questions regarding Joshua and its PRO and Packing implementations.

References

Alfred V. Aho and Jeffrey D. Ullman. 1969. Syntax directed translations and the pushdown assembler. *J. Comput. Syst. Sci.*, 3(1):37–56.

Hala Almaghout, Jie Jiang, and Andy Way. 2011. Ccg contextual labels in hierarchical phrase-based smt. In *Proceedings of the 15th Annual Conference of the European Association for Machine Translation (EAMT-2011)*, May.

Stanley F. Chen and Joshua T. Goodman. 1998. An empirical study of smoothing techniques for language modeling. Technical Report TR-10-98, Computer Science Group, Harvard University.

Colin Cherry and George Foster. 2012. Batch tuning strategies for statistical machine translation. In *HLT-NAACL*, pages 427–436.

David Chiang. 2005. A hierarchical phrase-based model for statistical machine translation. In *Proceedings of the 43rd Annual Meeting of the ACL*, pages 263–270, June.

David Chiang. 2006. An introduction to synchronous grammars.

David Chiang. 2007. Hierarchical phrase-based translation. *Computational Linguistics*, 33(2):201–228.

David Chiang. 2010. Learning to translate with source and target syntax. In *Proceedings of the 48th Annual Meeting of the Association for Computational Linguistics*, pages 1443–1452.

Juri Ganitkevitch, Yuan Cao, Jonathan Weese, Matt Post, and Chris Callison-Burch. 2012. Joshua 4.0: Packing, pro, and paraphrases. In *Proceedings of the Seventh Workshop on Statistical Machine Translation*, pages 283–291, Montréal, Canada, June. Association for Computational Linguistics.

Hany Hassan, Khalil Sima'an, and Andy Way. 2007. Supertagged phrase-based statistical machine translation. In *Proceedings of ACL 2007*, page 288295.

Hieu Hoang, Alexandra Birch, Chris Callison-burch, Richard Zens, Rwth Aachen, Alexandra Constantin, Marcello Federico, Nicola Bertoldi, Chris Dyer, Brooke Cowan, Wade Shen, Christine Moran, and Ondrej Bojar. 2007. Moses: Open source toolkit for statistical machine translation. In *Proceedings of the 41st Annual Meeting on Association for Computational Linguistics - Volume 1*, pages 177–180.

Mark Hopkins and Jonathan May. 2011. Tuning as ranking. In *Proceedings of the Conference on Empirical Methods in Natural Language Processing*, pages 1352–1362.

Shankar Kumar and William Byrne. 2004. Minimum bayes-risk decoding for statistical machine translation. In *HLT-NAACL*, page 16917.

Zhifei Li, Jason Eisner, and Sanjeev Khudanpur. 2009. Variational decoding for statistical machine translation. In *Proceedings of the Joint Conference of the 47th Annual Meeting of the ACL and the 4th International Joint Conference on Natural Language Processing of the AFNLP: Volume 2 - Volume 2*, pages 593–601.

Junhui Li, Zhaopeng Tu, Guodong Zhou, and Josef van Genabith. 2012. Using syntactic head information in hierarchical phrase-based translation. In *Proceedings of the Seventh Workshop on Statistical Machine Translation*, pages 232–242.

Yuval Marton, David Chiang, and Philip Resnik. 2012. Soft syntactic constraints for arabic—english hierarchical phrase-based translation. *Machine Translation*, 26(1-2):137–157.

Markos Mylonakis and Khalil Sima'an. 2011. Learning hierarchical translation structure with linguistic annotations. In *Proceedings of the 49th Annual Meeting of the Association for Computational Linguistics: Human Language Technologies*, pages 642–652.

Markos Mylonakis. 2012. *Learning the Latent Structure of Translation*. Ph.D. thesis, University of Amsterdam.

Franz Josef Och. 2003. Minimum error rate training in statistical machine translation. In *Proceedings of the 41st Annual Meeting on Association for Computational Linguistics - Volume 1*, pages 160–167.

Khalil Sima'an and Gideon Maillette de Buy Wenniger. 2011. Hierarchical translation equivalence over word alignments. Technical Report PP-2011-38, Institute for Logic, Language and Computation.

Roy W. Tromble, Shankar Kumar, Franz Och, and Wolfgang Macherey. 2008. Lattice minimum bayes-risk decoding for statistical machine translation. In *Proceedings of the Conference on Empirical Methods in Natural Language Processing*, pages 620–629.

Ashish Venugopal, Andreas Zollmann, Noah A. Smith, and Stephan Vogel. 2009. Preference grammars: softening syntactic constraints to improve statistical machine translation. In *Proceedings of Human Language Technologies: The 2009 Annual Conference of the North American Chapter of the Association for Computational Linguistics*, pages 236–244.

Dekai Wu. 1997. Stochastic inversion transduction grammars and bilingual parsing of parallel corpora. *Computational Linguistics*, 23:377–404.

Hao Zhang, Daniel Gildea, and David Chiang. 2008. Extracting synchronous grammar rules from word-level alignments in linear time. In *Proceedings of the 22nd International Conference on Computational Linguistics - Volume 1*, pages 1081–1088.

Andreas Zollmann and Ashish Venugopal. 2006. Syntax augmented machine translation via chart parsing. In

NAACL 2006 - Workshop on statistical machine translation, June.

Andreas Zollmann. 2011. *Learning Multiple-Nonterminal Synchronous Grammars for Statistical Machine Translation*. Ph.D. thesis, Carnegie Mellon University.

A Performance Study of Cube Pruning for Large-Scale Hierarchical Machine Translation

Matthias Huck[1] and **David Vilar**[2] and **Markus Freitag**[1] and **Hermann Ney**[1]

[1] Human Language Technology and Pattern Recognition Group, RWTH Aachen University
D-52056 Aachen, Germany
<surname>@cs.rwth-aachen.de

[2] DFKI GmbH
Alt-Moabit 91c
D-10559 Berlin, Germany
david.vilar@dfki.de

Abstract

In this paper, we empirically investigate the impact of critical configuration parameters in the popular cube pruning algorithm for decoding in hierarchical statistical machine translation. Specifically, we study how the choice of the k-best generation size affects translation quality and resource requirements in hierarchical search. We furthermore examine the influence of two different granularities of hypothesis recombination. Our experiments are conducted on the large-scale Chinese→English and Arabic→English NIST translation tasks. Besides standard hierarchical grammars, we also explore search with restricted recursion depth of hierarchical rules based on shallow-1 grammars.

1 Introduction

Cube pruning (Chiang, 2007) is a widely used search strategy in state-of-the-art hierarchical decoders. Some alternatives and extensions to the classical algorithm as proposed by David Chiang have been presented in the literature since, e.g. cube growing (Huang and Chiang, 2007), lattice-based hierarchical translation (Iglesias et al., 2009b; de Gispert et al., 2010), and source cardinality synchronous cube pruning (Vilar and Ney, 2012). Standard cube pruning remains the commonly adopted decoding procedure in hierarchical machine translation research at the moment, though. The algorithm has meanwhile been implemented in many publicly available toolkits, as for example in Moses (Koehn et al., 2007; Hoang et al., 2009), Joshua (Li et al., 2009a), Jane (Vilar et al., 2010), cdec (Dyer et al., 2010), Kriya (Sankaran et al., 2012), and NiuTrans (Xiao et al., 2012). While the plain hierarchical approach to machine translation (MT) is only formally syntax-based, cube pruning can also be utilized for decoding with syntactically or semantically enhanced models, for instance those by Venugopal et al. (2009), Shen et al. (2010), Xie et al. (2011), Almaghout et al. (2012), Li et al. (2012), Williams and Koehn (2012), or Baker et al. (2010).

Here, we look into the following key aspects of hierarchical phrase-based translation with cube pruning:

- Deep vs. shallow grammar.
- k-best generation size.
- Hypothesis recombination scheme.

We conduct a comparative study of all combinations of these three factors in hierarchical decoding and present detailed experimental analyses with respect to translation quality and search efficiency. We focus on two tasks which are of particular interest to the research community: the Chinese→English and Arabic→English NIST OpenMT translation tasks.

The paper is structured as follows: We briefly outline some important related work in the following section. We subsequently give a summary of the grammars used in hierarchical phrase-based translation, including a presentation of the difference between a deep and a shallow-1 grammar (Section 3). Essential aspects of hierarchical search with the cube pruning algorithm are explained in Section 4. We show how the k-best generation size is defined (we apply the limit without counting recombined candidates), and we present the two different hypothesis recombination schemes (*recombination T* and *recombination LM*). Our empirical investigations and findings constitute the major part of this work: In Section 5, we first accurately describe our setup, then conduct a number of comparative experiments with varied parameters on the two translation tasks, and finally analyze and discuss the results. We conclude the paper in Section 6.

2 Related Work

Hierarchical phrase-based translation (HPBT) was first proposed by Chiang (2005). Chiang also introduced the cube pruning algorithm for hierarchical search (Chiang, 2007). It is basically an adaptation of one of the k-best parsing algorithms by Huang and Chiang (2005). Good descriptions of the cube pruning implementation in the Joshua decoder have been provided by Li and Khudanpur (2008) and Li et al. (2009b). Xu and Koehn (2012) implemented hierarchical search with the cube growing algorithm in Moses and compared its performance to Moses' cube pruning implementation. Heafield et al. recently developed techniques to speed up hierarchical search by means of an improved language model integration (Heafield et al., 2011; Heafield et al., 2012; Heafield et al., 2013).

3 Probabilistic SCFGs for HPBT

In hierarchical phrase-based translation, a probabilistic synchronous context-free grammar (SCFG) is induced from a bilingual text. In addition to continuous *lexical* phrases, *hierarchical* phrases with usually up to two gaps are extracted from the word-aligned parallel training data.

Deep grammar. The non-terminal set of a standard hierarchical grammar comprises two symbols which are shared by source and target: the initial symbol S and one generic non-terminal symbol X. Extracted rules of a standard hierarchical grammar are of the form $X \rightarrow \langle \alpha, \beta, ^{\sim} \rangle$ where $\langle \alpha, \beta \rangle$ is a bilingual phrase pair that may contain X, i.e. $\alpha \in (\{X\} \cup V_F)^+$ and $\beta \in (\{X\} \cup V_E)^+$, where V_F and V_E are the source and target vocabulary, respectively. The $^{\sim}$ relation denotes a one-to-one correspondence between the non-terminals in α and in β. A non-lexicalized initial rule and a special glue rule complete the grammar. We denote standard hierarchical grammars as *deep* grammars here.

Shallow-1 grammar. Iglesias et al. (2009a) propose a limitation of the recursion depth for hierarchical rules with shallow grammars. In a *shallow-1* grammar, the generic non-terminal X of the standard hierarchical approach is replaced by two distinct non-terminals XH and XP. By changing the left-hand sides of the rules, lexical phrases are allowed to be derived from XP only, hierarchical phrases from XH only. On all right-hand sides of hierarchical rules, the X is replaced by XP. Gaps within hierarchical phrases can thus be filled with continuous lexical phrases only, not with hierarchical phrases. The initial and glue rules are adjusted accordingly.

4 Hierarchical Search with Cube Pruning

Hierarchical search is typically carried out with a parsing-based procedure. The parsing algorithm is extended to handle translation candidates and to incorporate language model scores via cube pruning.

The cube pruning algorithm. Cube pruning operates on a hypergraph which represents the whole parsing space. This hypergraph is built employing a customized version of the CYK+ parsing algorithm (Chappelier and Rajman, 1998). Given the hypergraph, cube pruning expands at most k derivations at each hypernode.[1] The pseudocode of the k-best generation step of the cube pruning algorithm is shown in Figure 1. This function is called in bottom-up topological order for all hypernodes. A heap of active derivations A is maintained. A initially contains the first-best derivations for each incoming hyperedge (line 1). Active derivations are processed in a loop (line 3) until a limit k is reached or A is empty. If a candidate derivation d is recombinable, the RECOMBINE auxiliary function recombines it and returns `true`; otherwise (for non-recombinable candidates) RECOMBINE returns `false`. Non-recombinable candidates are appended to the list D of k-best derivations (line 6). This list will be sorted before the function terminates

[1]The hypergraph on which cube pruning operates can be constructed based on other techniques, such as tree automata, but CYK+ parsing is the dominant approach.

(line 8). The PUSHSUCC auxiliary function (line 7) updates A with the next best derivations following d along the hyperedge. PUSHSUCC determines the cube order by processing adjacent derivations in a specific sequence (of predecessor hypernodes along the hyperedge and phrase translation options).[2]

k-best generation size. Candidate derivations are generated by cube pruning best-first along the incoming hyperedges. A problem results from the language model integration, though: As soon as language model context is considered, monotonicity properties of the derivation cost can no longer be guaranteed. Thus, even for single-best translation, k-best derivations are collected to a buffer in a beam search manner and finally sorted according to their cost. The k-best generation size is consequently a crucial parameter to the cube pruning algorithm.

Hypothesis recombination. Partial hypotheses with states that are indistinguishable from each other are recombined during search. We define two notions of when to consider two derivations as indistinguishable, and thus when to recombine them:

Recombination T. The T recombination scheme recombines derivations that produce identical translations.

Recombination LM. The LM recombination scheme recombines derivations with identical language model context.

Recombination is conducted within the loop of the k-best generation step of cube pruning. Recombined derivations do not increment the generation count; the k-best generation limit is thus effectively applied after recombination.[3] In general, more phrase translation candidates per hypernode are being considered (and need to be rated with the language model) in the *recombination LM* scheme compared to the *recombination T* scheme. The more partial hypotheses can be recombined, the more iterations of the inner code block of the k-best generation loop are possible. The same internal k-best generation size results in a larger search space for *recombination LM*. We will examine how the overall number of loop iterations relates to the k-best generation limit. By measuring the number of derivations as well as the number of recombination operations on our test sets, we will be able to give an insight into how large the fraction of recombinable candidates is for different configurations.

Input: a hypernode and the size k of the k-best list
Output: D, a list with the k-best derivations

```
1 let A ← heap({(e, 1_|e|) | e ∈ incoming edges)})
2 let D ← []
3 while |A| > 0 ∧ |D| < k do
4     d ← pop(A)
5     if not RECOMBINE(D, d) then
6         D ← D ++ [d]
7     PUSHSUCC(d, A)
8 sort D
```

Figure 1: k-best generation with the cube pruning algorithm.

5 Experiments

We conduct experiments which evaluate performance in terms of both translation quality and computational efficiency, i.e. translation speed and memory consumption, for combinations of deep or shallow-1 grammars with the two hypothesis recombination schemes and an exhaustive range of k-best generation size settings. Empirical results are presented on the Chinese→English and Arabic→English 2008 NIST tasks (NIST, 2008).

5.1 Experimental Setup

We work with parallel training corpora of 3.0 M Chinese–English sentence pairs (77.5 M Chinese / 81.0 M English running words after preprocessing) and 2.5 M Arabic–English sentence pairs (54.3 M Arabic / 55.3 M English running words after preprocessing), respectively. Word alignments are created by aligning the data in both directions with GIZA++ and symmetrizing the two trained alignments (Och and Ney, 2003). When extracting phrases, we apply several restrictions, in particular a maximum length of ten on source and target side for lexical phrases, a length limit of five on source and ten on target side for hierarchical phrases (including non-terminal symbols), and no more than two gaps per phrase.

[2] See Vilar (2011) for the pseudocode of the PUSHSUCC function and other details which are omitted here.

[3] Whether recombined derivations contribute to the generation count or not is a configuration decision (or implementation decision). Please note that some publicly available toolkits count recombined derivations by default.

Table 1: Data statistics for the test sets. Numbers have been replaced by a special category symbol.

	Chinese MT08	Arabic MT08
Sentences	1 357	1 360
Running words	34 463	45 095
Vocabulary	6 209	9 387

The decoder loads only the best translation options per distinct source side with respect to the weighted phrase-level model scores (100 for Chinese, 50 for Arabic). The language models are 4-grams with modified Kneser-Ney smoothing (Kneser and Ney, 1995; Chen and Goodman, 1998) which have been trained with the SRILM toolkit (Stolcke, 2002).

During decoding, a maximum length constraint of ten is applied to all non-terminals except the initial symbol S. Model weights are optimized with MERT (Och, 2003) on 100-best lists. The optimized weights are obtained (separately for deep and for shallow-1 grammars) with a k-best generation size of 1 000 for Chinese→English and of 500 for Arabic→English and kept for all setups. We employ MT06 as development sets. Translation quality is measured in truecase with BLEU (Papineni et al., 2002) on the MT08 test sets. Data statistics for the preprocessed source sides of both the Chinese→English MT08 test set and the Arabic→English MT08 test set are given in Table 1.

Our translation experiments are conducted with the open source translation toolkit Jane (Vilar et al., 2010; Vilar et al., 2012). The core implementation of the toolkit is written in C++. We compiled with GCC version 4.4.3 using its `-O2` optimization flag. We employ the SRILM libraries to perform language model scoring in the decoder. In binarized version, the language models have a size of 3.6G (Chinese→English) and 6.2G (Arabic→English). Language models and phrase tables have been copied to the local hard disks of the machines. In all experiments, the language model is completely loaded beforehand. Loading time of the language model and any other initialization steps are not included in the measured translation time. Phrase tables are in the Jane toolkit's binarized format. The decoder initializes the prefix tree structure, required nodes get loaded from secondary storage into main memory on demand, and the loaded content is being cleared each time a new input sentence is to be parsed. There is nearly no overhead due to unused data in main memory. We do not rely on memory mapping. Memory statistics are with respect to virtual memory. The hardware was equipped with RAM well beyond the requirements of the tasks, and sufficient memory has been reserved for the processes.

5.2 Experimental Results

Figures 2 and 3 depict how the Chinese→English and Arabic→English setups behave in terms of translation quality. The k-best generation size in cube pruning is varied between 10 and 10 000. The four graphs in each plot illustrate the results with combinations of deep grammar and recombination scheme T, deep grammar and recombination scheme LM, shallow grammar and recombination scheme T, as well as shallow grammar and recombination scheme LM. Figures 4 and 5 show the corresponding translation speed in words per second for these settings. The maximum memory requirements in gigabytes are given in Figures 6 and 7. In order to visualize the trade-offs between translation quality and resource consumption somewhat better, we plotted translation quality against time requirements in Figures 8 and 9 and translation quality against memory requirements in Figures 10 and 11. Translation quality and model score (averaged over all sentences; higher is better) are nicely correlated for all configurations, as can be concluded from Figures 12 through 15.

5.3 Discussion

Chinese→English. For Chinese→English translation, the system with deep grammar performs generally a bit better with respect to quality than the shallow one, which accords with the findings of other groups (de Gispert et al., 2010; Sankaran et al., 2012). The LM recombination scheme yields slightly better quality than the T scheme, and with the shallow-1 grammar it outperforms the T scheme at any given fixed amount of time or memory allocation (Figures 8 and 10).

Shallow-1 translation is up to roughly 2.5 times faster than translation with the deep grammar. However, the shallow-1 setups are considerably slowed down at higher k-best sizes as well, while the effort pays off only very moderately. Overall, the

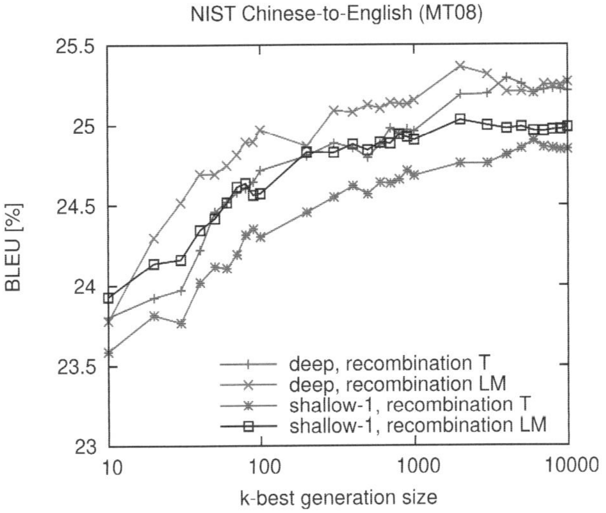

Figure 2: Chinese→English translation quality (truecase).

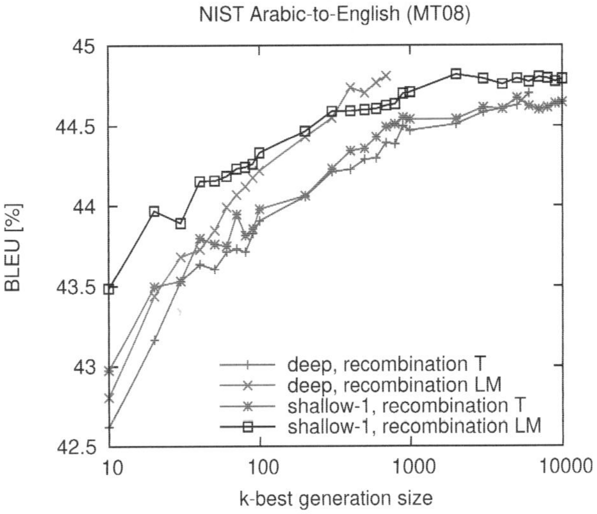

Figure 3: Arabic→English translation quality (truecase).

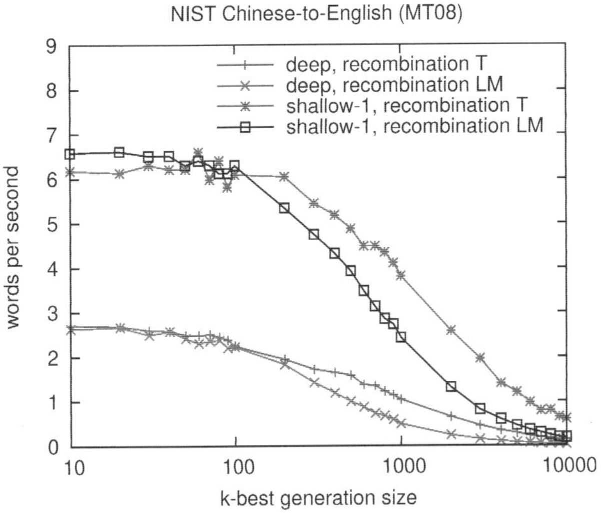

Figure 4: Chinese→English translation speed.

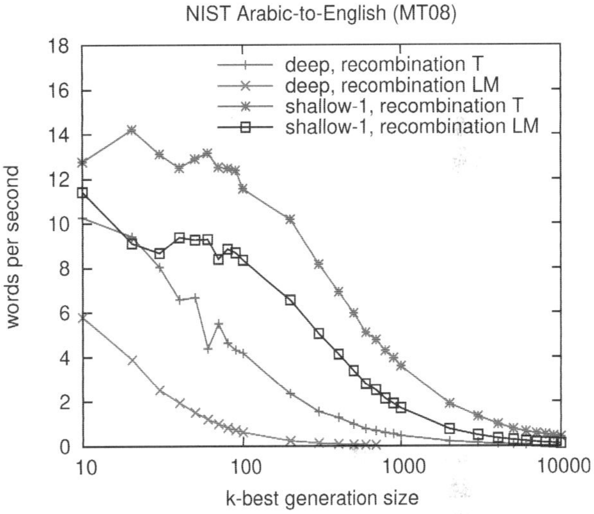

Figure 5: Arabic→English translation speed.

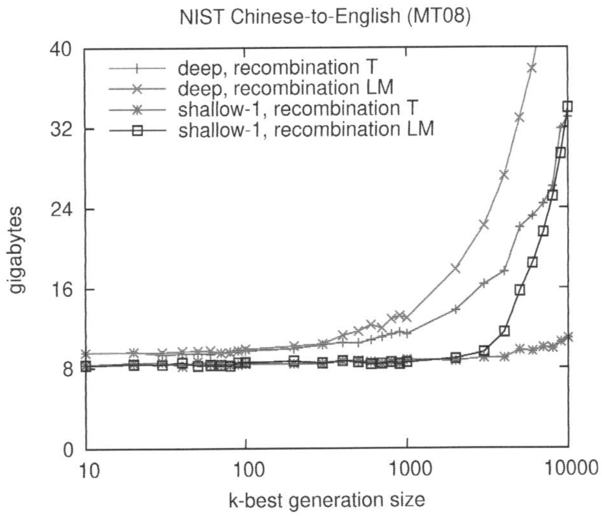

Figure 6: Chinese→English memory requirements.

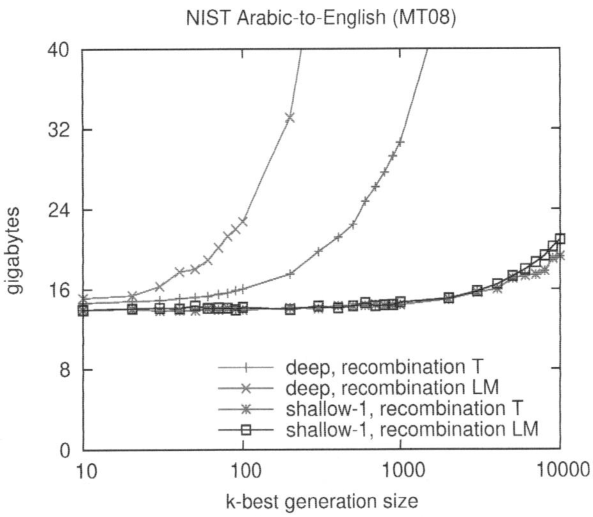

Figure 7: Arabic→English memory requirements.

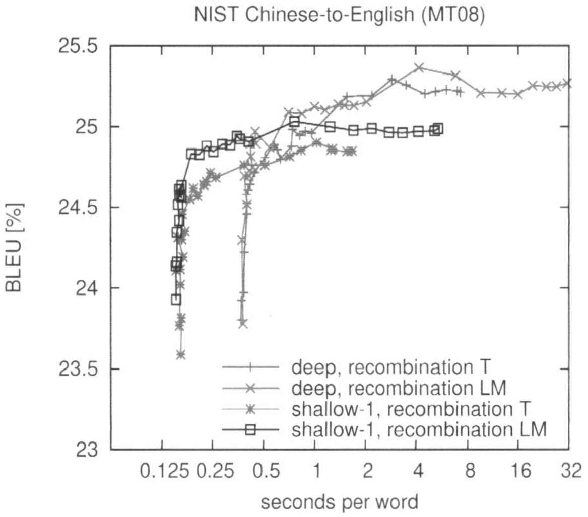

Figure 8: Trade-off between translation quality and speed for Chinese→English.

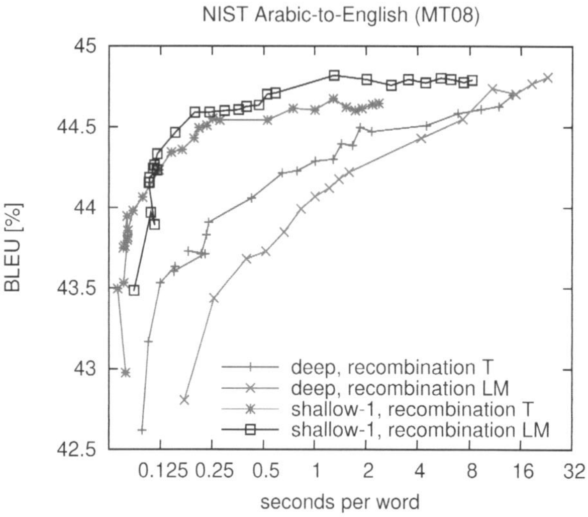

Figure 9: Trade-off between translation quality and speed for Arabic→English.

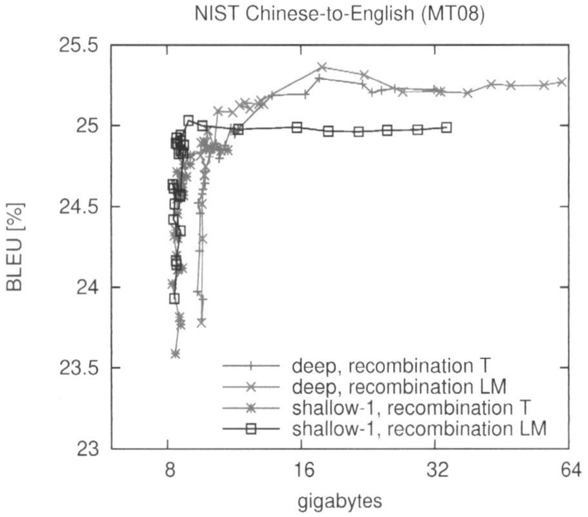

Figure 10: Trade-off between translation quality and memory requirements for Chinese→English.

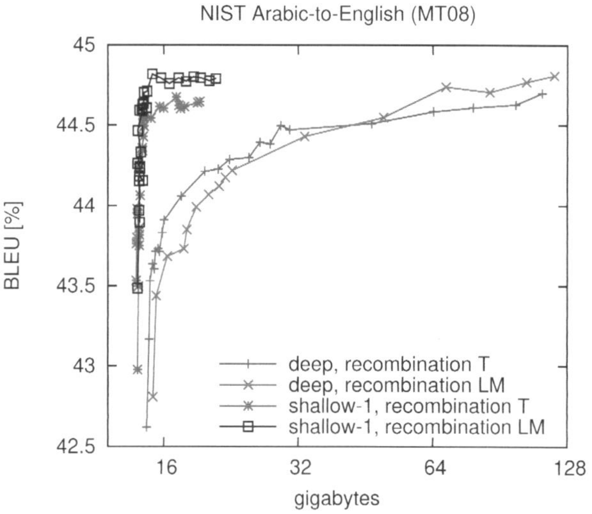

Figure 11: Trade-off between translation quality and memory requirements for Arabic→English.

shallow-1 grammar at a k-best size between 100 and 1 000 seems to offer a good compromise of quality and efficiency. Deep translation with $k = 2\,000$ and the LM recombination scheme promises high quality translation, but note the rapid memory consumption increase beyond $k = 1\,000$ with the deep grammar. At $k \leq 1\,000$, memory consumption is not an issue in both deep and shallow systems, but translation speed starts to drop at $k > 100$ already.

Arabic→English. Shallow-1 translation produces competitive quality for Arabic→English translation (de Gispert et al., 2010; Huck et al., 2011). The LM recombination scheme boosts the BLEU scores slightly. The systems with deep grammar are slowed down strongly with every increase of the k-best size. Their memory consumption likewise inflates early. We actually stopped running experiments with deep grammars for Arabic→English at $k = 7\,000$ for the T recombination scheme, and at $k = 700$ for the LM recombination scheme because 124G of memory did not suffice any more for higher k-best sizes. The memory consumption of the shallow systems stays nearly constant across a large range of the surveyed k-best sizes, but Figure 11 reveals a plateau where more resources do not improve translation quality. Increasing k from 100 to 2 000 in the shallow setup with LM recombination provides half a BLEU point, but reduces speed by a factor of more than 10.

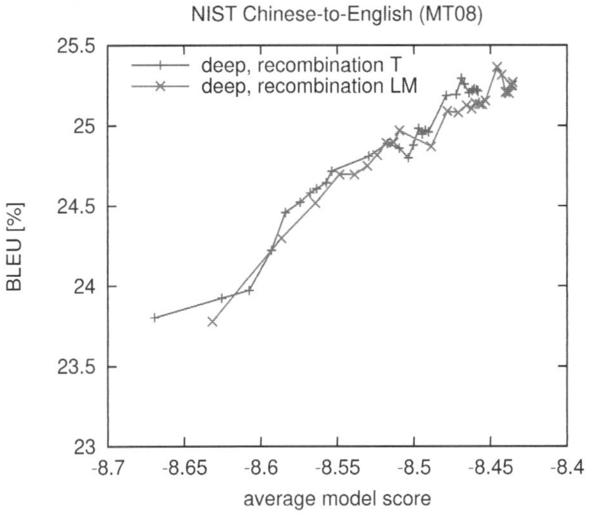

Figure 12: Relation of translation quality and average model score for Chinese→English (deep grammar).

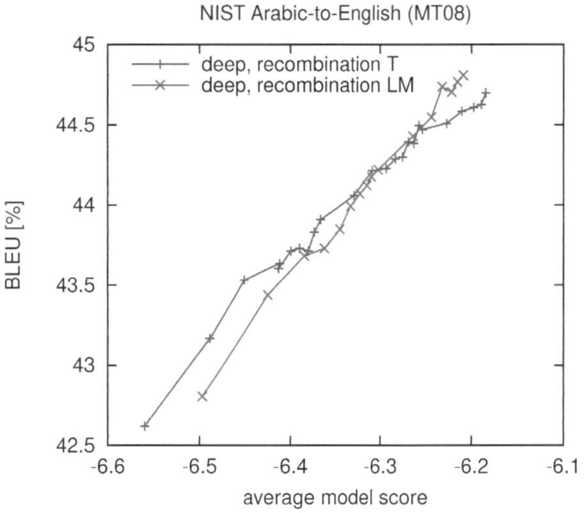

Figure 13: Relation of translation quality and average model score for Arabic→English (deep grammar).

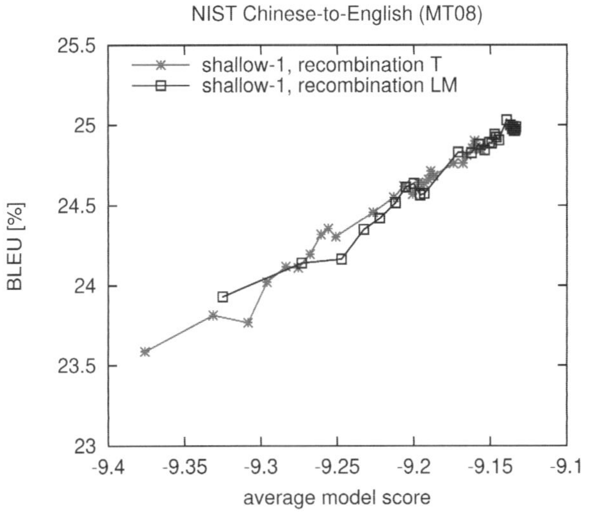

Figure 14: Relation of translation quality and average model score for Chinese→English (shallow-1 grammar).

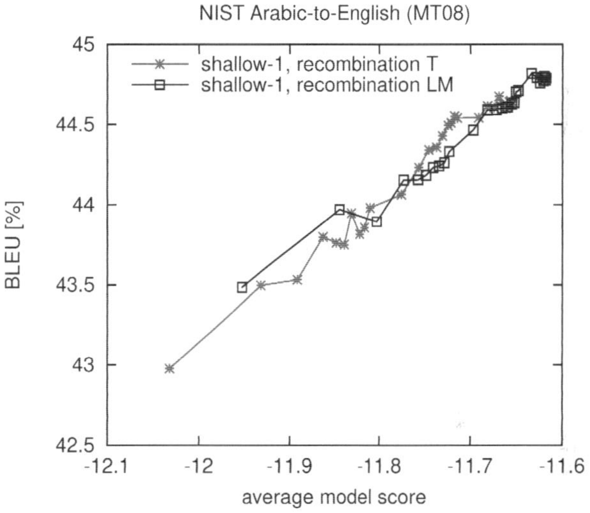

Figure 15: Relation of translation quality and average model score for Arabic→English (shallow-1 grammar).

Actual amount of derivations. We measured the amount of hypernodes (Table 2), the amount of actually generated derivations after recombination, and the amount of generated candidate derivations including recombined ones—or, equivalently, loop iterations in the algorithm from Figure 1—for selected limits k (Tables 3 and 4). The ratio of the average amount of derivations per hypernode after and before recombination remains consistently at low values for all recombination T setups. For the setups with LM recombination scheme, this recombination factor rises with larger k, i.e. the fraction of recombinable candidates increases. The increase is remarkably pronounced for Arabic→English with deep grammar. The steep slope of the recombination factor may be interpreted as an indicator for undesired overgeneration of the deep grammar on the Arabic→English task.

6 Conclusion

We systematically studied three key aspects of hierarchical phrase-based translation with cube pruning: Deep vs. shallow-1 grammars, the k-best generation size, and the hypothesis recombination scheme. In a series of empirical experiments, we revealed the trade-offs between translation quality and resource requirements to a more fine-grained degree than this is typically done in the literature.

Table 2: Average amount of hypernodes per sentence and average length of the preprocessed input sentences on the NIST Chinese→English (MT08) and Arabic→English (MT08) tasks.

	Chinese→English		Arabic→English	
	deep	**shallow-1**	**deep**	**shallow-1**
avg. #hypernodes per sentence	480.5	200.7	896.4	308.4
avg. source sentence length	25.4		33.2	

Table 3: Detailed statistics about the actual amount of derivations on the NIST Chinese→English task (MT08).

	deep					
	recombination T			**recombination LM**		
k	avg. #derivations per hypernode (after recombination)	avg. #derivations per hypernode (incl. recombined)	factor	avg. #derivations per hypernode (after recombination)	avg. #derivations per hypernode (incl. recombined)	factor
10	10.0	11.7	1.17	10.0	18.2	1.82
100	99.9	120.1	1.20	99.9	275.8	2.76
1000	950.1	1142.3	1.20	950.1	4246.9	4.47
10000	9429.8	11262.8	1.19	9418.1	72008.4	7.65

	shallow-1					
	recombination T			**recombination LM**		
k	avg. #derivations per hypernode (after recombination)	avg. #derivations per hypernode (incl. recombined)	factor	avg. #derivations per hypernode (after recombination)	avg. #derivations per hypernode (incl. recombined)	factor
10	9.7	11.3	1.17	9.6	13.6	1.41
100	90.8	105.2	1.16	90.4	168.6	1.86
1000	707.3	811.3	1.15	697.4	2143.4	3.07
10000	6478.1	7170.4	1.11	6202.8	34165.6	5.51

Table 4: Detailed statistics about the actual amount of derivations on the NIST Arabic→English task (MT08).

	deep					
	recombination T			**recombination LM**		
k	avg. #derivations per hypernode (after recombination)	avg. #derivations per hypernode (incl. recombined)	factor	avg. #derivations per hypernode (after recombination)	avg. #derivations per hypernode (incl. recombined)	factor
10	10.0	18.3	1.83	10.0	71.5	7.15
100	98.0	177.4	1.81	98.0	1726.0	17.62
500	482.1	849.0	1.76	482.1	14622.1	30.33
1000	961.8	1675.0	1.74	–	–	–

	shallow-1					
	recombination T			**recombination LM**		
k	avg. #derivations per hypernode (after recombination)	avg. #derivations per hypernode (incl. recombined)	factor	avg. #derivations per hypernode (after recombination)	avg. #derivations per hypernode (incl. recombined)	factor
10	9.6	12.1	1.26	9.6	16.6	1.73
100	80.9	105.2	1.30	80.2	193.8	2.42
1000	690.1	902.1	1.31	672.1	2413.0	3.59
10000	5638.6	7149.5	1.27	5275.1	31283.6	5.93

Acknowledgments

This work was partly achieved as part of the Quaero Programme, funded by OSEO, French State agency for innovation. This material is also partly based upon work supported by the DARPA BOLT project under Contract No. HR0011-12-C-0015. Any opinions, findings and conclusions or recommendations expressed in this material are those of the authors and do not necessarily reflect the views of the DARPA. The research leading to these results has received funding from the European Union Seventh Framework Programme (FP7/2007-2013) under grant agreement n° 287658.

References

Hala Almaghout, Jie Jiang, and Andy Way. 2012. Extending CCG-based Syntactic Constraints in Hierarchical Phrase-Based SMT. In *Proc. of the Annual Conf. of the European Assoc. for Machine Translation (EAMT)*, pages 193–200, Trento, Italy, May.

Kathryn Baker, Michael Bloodgood, Chris Callison-Burch, Bonnie Dorr, Nathaniel Filardo, Lori Levin, Scott Miller, and Christine Piatko. 2010. Semantically-Informed Syntactic Machine Translation: A Tree-Grafting Approach. In *Proc. of the Conf. of the Assoc. for Machine Translation in the Americas (AMTA)*, Denver, CO, USA, October/November.

Jean-Cédric Chappelier and Martin Rajman. 1998. A Generalized CYK Algorithm for Parsing Stochastic CFG. In *Proc. of the First Workshop on Tabulation in Parsing and Deduction*, pages 133–137, Paris, France, April.

Stanley F. Chen and Joshua Goodman. 1998. An Empirical Study of Smoothing Techniques for Language Modeling. Technical Report TR-10-98, Computer Science Group, Harvard University, Cambridge, MA, USA, August.

David Chiang. 2005. A Hierarchical Phrase-Based Model for Statistical Machine Translation. In *Proc. of the Annual Meeting of the Assoc. for Computational Linguistics (ACL)*, pages 263–270, Ann Arbor, MI, USA, June.

David Chiang. 2007. Hierarchical Phrase-Based Translation. *Computational Linguistics*, 33(2):201–228, June.

Adrià de Gispert, Gonzalo Iglesias, Graeme Blackwood, Eduardo R. Banga, and William Byrne. 2010. Hierarchical Phrase-Based Translation with Weighted Finite-State Transducers and Shallow-n Grammars. *Computational Linguistics*, 36(3):505–533.

Chris Dyer, Adam Lopez, Juri Ganitkevitch, Johnathan Weese, Ferhan Ture, Phil Blunsom, Hendra Setiawan, Vladimir Eidelman, and Philip Resnik. 2010. cdec: A Decoder, Alignment, and Learning framework for finite-state and context-free translation models. In *Proc. of the ACL 2010 System Demonstrations*, pages 7–12, Uppsala, Sweden, July.

Kenneth Heafield, Hieu Hoang, Philipp Koehn, Tetsuo Kiso, and Marcello Federico. 2011. Left Language Model State for Syntactic Machine Translation. In *Proc. of the Int. Workshop on Spoken Language Translation (IWSLT)*, pages 183–190, San Francisco, CA, USA, December.

Kenneth Heafield, Philipp Koehn, and Alon Lavie. 2012. Language Model Rest Costs and Space-Efficient Storage. In *Proc. of the 2012 Joint Conf. on Empirical Methods in Natural Language Processing and Computational Natural Language Learning*, EMNLP-CoNLL '12, pages 1169–1178, Jeju Island, Korea, July.

Kenneth Heafield, Philipp Koehn, and Alon Lavie. 2013. Grouping Language Model Boundary Words to Speed K-Best Extraction from Hypergraphs. In *Proc. of the Human Language Technology Conf. / North American Chapter of the Assoc. for Computational Linguistics (HLT-NAACL)*, Atlanta, GA, USA, June.

Hieu Hoang, Philipp Koehn, and Adam Lopez. 2009. A Unified Framework for Phrase-Based, Hierarchical, and Syntax-Based Statistical Machine Translation. In *Proc. of the Int. Workshop on Spoken Language Translation (IWSLT)*, pages 152–159, Tokyo, Japan, December.

Liang Huang and David Chiang. 2005. Better k-best Parsing. In *Proc. of the 9th Int. Workshop on Parsing Technologies*, pages 53–64, October.

Liang Huang and David Chiang. 2007. Forest Rescoring: Faster Decoding with Integrated Language Models. In *Proc. of the Annual Meeting of the Assoc. for Computational Linguistics (ACL)*, pages 144–151, Prague, Czech Republic, June.

Matthias Huck, David Vilar, Daniel Stein, and Hermann Ney. 2011. Advancements in Arabic-to-English Hierarchical Machine Translation. In *15th Annual Conference of the European Association for Machine Translation*, pages 273–280, Leuven, Belgium, May.

Gonzalo Iglesias, Adrià de Gispert, Eduardo R. Banga, and William Byrne. 2009a. Rule Filtering by Pattern for Efficient Hierarchical Translation. In *Proc. of the 12th Conf. of the Europ. Chapter of the Assoc. for Computational Linguistics (EACL)*, pages 380–388, Athens, Greece, March.

Gonzalo Iglesias, Adrià de Gispert, Eduardo R. Banga, and William Byrne. 2009b. Hierarchical Phrase-Based Translation with Weighted Finite State Transducers. In *Proc. of the Human Language Technology Conf. / North American Chapter of the Assoc. for Computational Linguistics (HLT-NAACL)*, pages 433–441, Boulder, CO, USA, June.

Reinhard Kneser and Hermann Ney. 1995. Improved Backing-Off for M-gram Language Modeling. In *Proc. of the International Conf. on Acoustics, Speech, and Signal Processing*, volume 1, pages 181–184, Detroit, MI, USA, May.

P. Koehn, H. Hoang, A. Birch, C. Callison-Burch, M. Federico, N. Bertoldi, B. Cowan, W. Shen, C. Moran, R. Zens, C. Dyer, O. Bojar, A. Constantin, and E. Herbst. 2007. Moses: Open Source Toolkit for Statistical Machine Translation. In *Proc. of the Annual Meeting of the Assoc. for Computational Linguistics (ACL)*, pages 177–180, Prague, Czech Republic, June.

Zhifei Li and Sanjeev Khudanpur. 2008. A Scalable Decoder for Parsing-Based Machine Translation with Equivalent Language Model State Maintenance. In *Proceedings of the Second Workshop on Syntax and Structure in Statistical Translation*, SSST '08, pages 10–18, Columbus, OH, USA, June.

Zhifei Li, Chris Callison-Burch, Chris Dyer, Sanjeev Khudanpur, Lane Schwartz, Wren Thornton, Jonathan Weese, and Omar Zaidan. 2009a. Joshua: An Open Source Toolkit for Parsing-Based Machine Translation. In *Proc. of the Workshop on Statistical Machine Translation (WMT)*, pages 135–139, Athens, Greece, March.

Zhifei Li, Chris Callison-Burch, Sanjeev Khudanpur, and Wren Thornton. 2009b. Decoding in Joshua: Open Source, Parsing-Based Machine Translation. *The Prague Bulletin of Mathematical Linguistics*, (91):47–56, January.

Junhui Li, Zhaopeng Tu, Guodong Zhou, and Josef van Genabith. 2012. Using Syntactic Head Information in Hierarchical Phrase-Based Translation. In *Proc. of the Workshop on Statistical Machine Translation (WMT)*, pages 232–242, Montréal, Canada, June.

NIST. 2008. Open Machine Translation 2008 Evaluation. `http://www.itl.nist.gov/iad/mig/tests/mt/2008/`.

Franz Josef Och and Hermann Ney. 2003. A Systematic Comparison of Various Statistical Alignment Models. *Computational Linguistics*, 29(1):19–51, March.

Franz Josef Och. 2003. Minimum Error Rate Training for Statistical Machine Translation. In *Proc. of the Annual Meeting of the Assoc. for Computational Linguistics (ACL)*, pages 160–167, Sapporo, Japan, July.

Kishore Papineni, Salim Roukos, Todd Ward, and Wei-Jing Zhu. 2002. Bleu: a Method for Automatic Evaluation of Machine Translation. In *Proc. of the Annual Meeting of the Assoc. for Computational Linguistics (ACL)*, pages 311–318, Philadelphia, PA, USA, July.

Baskaran Sankaran, Majid Razmara, and Anoop Sarkar. 2012. Kriya - An end-to-end Hierarchical Phrase-based MT System. *The Prague Bulletin of Mathematical Linguistics*, (97):83–98, April.

Libin Shen, Jinxi Xu, and Ralph Weischedel. 2010. String-to-Dependency Statistical Machine Translation. *Computational Linguistics*, 36(4):649–671, December.

Andreas Stolcke. 2002. SRILM – an Extensible Language Modeling Toolkit. In *Proc. of the Int. Conf. on Spoken Language Processing (ICSLP)*, volume 3, Denver, CO, USA, September.

Ashish Venugopal, Andreas Zollmann, Noah A. Smith, and Stephan Vogel. 2009. Preference Grammars: Softening Syntactic Constraints to Improve Statistical Machine Translation. In *Proc. of the Human Language Technology Conf. / North American Chapter of the Assoc. for Computational Linguistics (HLT-NAACL)*, pages 236–244, Boulder, CO, USA, June.

David Vilar and Hermann Ney. 2012. Cardinality pruning and language model heuristics for hierarchical phrase-based translation. *Machine Translation*, 26(3):217–254, September.

David Vilar, Daniel Stein, Matthias Huck, and Hermann Ney. 2010. Jane: Open Source Hierarchical Translation, Extended with Reordering and Lexicon Models. In *Proc. of the Workshop on Statistical Machine Translation (WMT)*, pages 262–270, Uppsala, Sweden, July.

David Vilar, Daniel Stein, Matthias Huck, and Hermann Ney. 2012. Jane: an advanced freely available hierarchical machine translation toolkit. *Machine Translation*, 26(3):197–216, September.

David Vilar. 2011. *Investigations on Hierarchical Phrase-Based Machine Translation*. Ph.D. thesis, RWTH Aachen University, Aachen, Germany, November.

Philip Williams and Philipp Koehn. 2012. GHKM Rule Extraction and Scope-3 Parsing in Moses. In *Proc. of the Workshop on Statistical Machine Translation (WMT)*, pages 388–394, Montréal, Canada, June.

Tong Xiao, Jingbo Zhu, Hao Zhang, and Qiang Li. 2012. NiuTrans: An Open Source Toolkit for Phrase-based and Syntax-based Machine Translation. In *Proc. of the ACL 2012 System Demonstrations*, pages 19–24, Jeju, Republic of Korea, July.

Jun Xie, Haitao Mi, and Qun Liu. 2011. A Novel Dependency-to-String Model for Statistical Machine Translation. In *Proc. of the Conf. on Empirical Methods for Natural Language Processing (EMNLP)*, pages 216–226, Edinburgh, Scotland, UK, July.

Wenduan Xu and Philipp Koehn. 2012. Extending Hiero Decoding in Moses with Cube Growing. *The Prague Bulletin of Mathematical Linguistics*, (98):133–142, October.

Combining Word Reordering Methods on different Linguistic Abstraction Levels for Statistical Machine Translation

Teresa Herrmann, Jan Niehues, Alex Waibel
Institute for Anthropomatics
Karlsruhe Institute of Technology
Karlsruhe, Germany
{teresa.herrmann,jan.niehues,alexander.waibel}@kit.edu

Abstract

We describe a novel approach to combining lexicalized, POS-based and syntactic tree-based word reordering in a phrase-based machine translation system. Our results show that each of the presented reordering methods leads to improved translation quality on its own. The strengths however can be combined to achieve further improvements. We present experiments on German-English and German-French translation. We report improvements of 0.7 BLEU points by adding tree-based and lexicalized reordering. Up to 1.1 BLEU points can be gained by POS and tree-based reordering over a baseline with lexicalized reordering. A human analysis, comparing subjective translation quality as well as a detailed error analysis show the impact of our presented tree-based rules in terms of improved sentence quality and reduction of errors related to missing verbs and verb positions.

1 Introduction

One of the main difficulties in statistical machine translation (SMT) is presented by the different word orders between languages. Most state-of-the-art phrase-based SMT systems handle it within phrase pairs or during decoding by allowing words to be swapped while translation hypotheses are generated. An additional reordering model might be included in the log-linear model of translation. However, these methods can cover reorderings only over a very limited distance. Recently, reordering as preprocessing has drawn much attention. The idea is to detach the reordering problem from the decoding process and to apply a reordering model prior to translation in order to facilitate a monotone translation.

Encouraged by the improvements that can be achieved with part-of-speech (POS) reordering rules (Niehues and Kolss, 2009; Rottmann and Vogel, 2007), we apply such rules on a different linguistic level. We abstract from the words in the sentence and learn reordering rules based on syntactic constituents in the source language sentence. Syntactic parse trees represent the sentence structure and show the relations between constituents in the sentence. Relying on syntactic constituents instead of POS tags should help to model the reordering task more reliably, since sentence constituents are moved as whole blocks of words, thus keeping the sentence structure intact.

In addition, we combine the POS-based and syntactic tree-based reordering models and also add a lexicalized reordering model, which is used in many state-of-the-art phrase-based SMT systems nowadays.

2 Related Work

The problem of word reordering has been addressed by several approaches over the last years.

In a phrase-based SMT system reordering can be achieved during decoding by allowing swaps of words within a defined window. Lexicalized reordering models (Koehn et al., 2005; Tillmann, 2004) include information about the orientation of adjacent phrases that is learned during phrase extraction. This reordering method, which affects the scoring of translation hypotheses but does not generate new reorderings, is used e.g. in the open source machine translation system Moses (Koehn et al., 2007).

Syntax-based (Yamada and Knight, 2001) or syntax-augmented (Zollmann and Venugopal, 2006) MT systems address the reordering problem by embedding syntactic analysis in the decoding process. Hierarchical MT systems (Chiang, 2005) construct a syntactic hierarchy during decoding, which is independent of linguistic categories.

To our best knowledge Xia and McCord (2004) were the first to model the word reordering problem as a preprocessing step. They automatically learn reordering rules for English-French translation from source and target language dependency trees. Afterwards, many followed these footsteps. Earlier approaches craft reordering rules manually based on syntactic or dependency parse trees or POS tags designed for particular languages (Collins et al., 2005; Popović and Ney, 2006; Habash, 2007; Wang et al., 2007). Later there were more and more approaches using data-driven methods. Costa-jussà and Fonollosa (2006) frame the word reordering problem as a translation task and use word class information to translate the original source sentence into a reordered source sentence that can be translated more easily. A very popular approach is to automatically learn reordering rules based on POS tags or syntactic chunks (Popović and Ney, 2006; Rottmann and Vogel, 2007; Zhang et al., 2007; Crego and Habash, 2008). Khalilov et al. (2009) present reordering rules learned from source and target side syntax trees. More recently, Genzel (2010) proposed to automatically learn reordering rules from IBM1 alignments and source side dependency trees. In DeNero and Uszkoreit (2011) no parser is needed, but the sentence structure used for learning the reordering model is induced automatically from a parallel corpus. Among these approaches most are able to cover short-range reorderings and some store reordering variants in a word lattice leaving the selection of the path to the decoder. Long-range reorderings are addressed by manual rules (Collins et al., 2005) or using automatically learned rules (Niehues and Kolss, 2009).

Motivated by the POS-based reordering models in Niehues and Kolss (2009) and Rottmann and Vogel (2007), we present a reordering model based on the syntactic structure of the source sentence. We intend to cover both short-range and long-range reordering more reliably by abstracting to constituents extracted from syntactic parse trees instead of working only with morphosyntactic information on the word level. Furthermore, we combine POS-based and tree-based models and additionally include a lexicalized reordering model. Altogether we apply word reordering on three different levels: lexicalized reordering model on the word level, POS-based reordering on the morphosyntactic level and syntax tree-based reordering on the constituent level. In contrast to previous work we use original syntactic parse trees instead of binarized parse trees or dependency trees. Furthermore, our goal is to address especially long-range reorderings involving verb constructions.

3 Motivation

When translating from German to English different word order is the most prominent problem. Especially the verb needs to be shifted over long distances in the sentence, since the position of the verb differs in German and English sentences. The finite verbs in the English language are generally located at the second position in the sentence. In German this is only the case in a main clause. In German subordinate clauses the verb is at the final position as shown in Example 1.

Example 1:

Source:	*..., nachdem ich eine Weile im Internet gesucht habe.*
Gloss:	*... after I a while in-the internet searched have.*
POS Reord.:	*..., nachdem ich habe eine Weile im Internet gesucht.*
POS Transl.:	*... as I have for some time on the Internet.*

The example shows first the source sentence and an English gloss. **POS Reord** presents the reordered source sentence as produced by POS rules. This should be the source sentence according to target language word order. **POS Transl** shows the translation of the reordered sequence. We can see that some cases remain unresolved. The POS rules succeed in putting the auxiliary *habe/have* to the right position in the sentence. But the participle, carrying the main meaning of the sentence, is not shifted together with the auxiliary. During translation it is dropped from the sentence, rendering it unintelligible.

A reason why the POS rules do not shift both parts of the verb might be that the rules operate on the word level only and treat every POS tag independently of the others. A reordering model based on syntactic constituents can help with this. Additional information about the syntactic structure of the sentence allows to identify which words belong together and should not be separated, but shifted as a whole block. Abstracting from the word level to the constituent level also provides the advantage that even though reorderings are performed over long sentence spans, the rules consist of less reordering units (constituents which themselves consist of constituents or words) and can be learned more reliably.

4 Tree-based Reordering

In order to encourage linguistically meaningful reorderings we learn rules based on syntactic tree constituents. While the POS-based rules are flat and perform the reordering on a sequence of words, the tree-based rules operate on subtrees in the parse tree as shown in Figure 1.

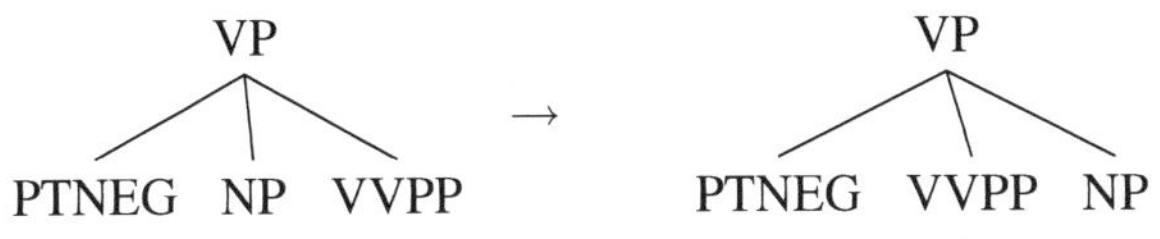

Figure 1: Example reordering rule based on subtrees

A syntactic parse tree contains both the word-level categories, i.e. parts-of-speech and higher order categories, i.e. constituents. In this way it provides information about the building blocks of a sentence that belong together and should not be taken apart by reordering. Consequently, the tree-based reordering operates both on the word level and on the constituent level to make use of all available information in the parse tree. It is able to handle long-range reorderings as well as short-range reorderings, depending on how many words the reordered constituents cover. The tree-based reordering rules should also be more stable and introduce less random word shuffling than the POS-based rules.

The reordering model consists of two stages. First the rule extraction, where the rules are learned by searching the training corpus for crossing alignments which indicate a reordering between source and target language. The second is the application of the learned reordering rules to the input text prior to translation.

4.1 Rule Extraction

As shown in Figure 4 we learn rules like this:

VP PTNEG NP VVPP → VP PTNEG VVPP NP

where the first item in the rule is the head node of the subtree and the rest represent the children. In the second part of the rule the children are indexed so that children of the same category cannot be confused. Figure 2 shows an example for rule extraction: a sentence in its syntactic parse tree representation, the sentence in the target language and an automatically generated alignment. A reordering occurs between the constituents *VVPP* and *NP*.

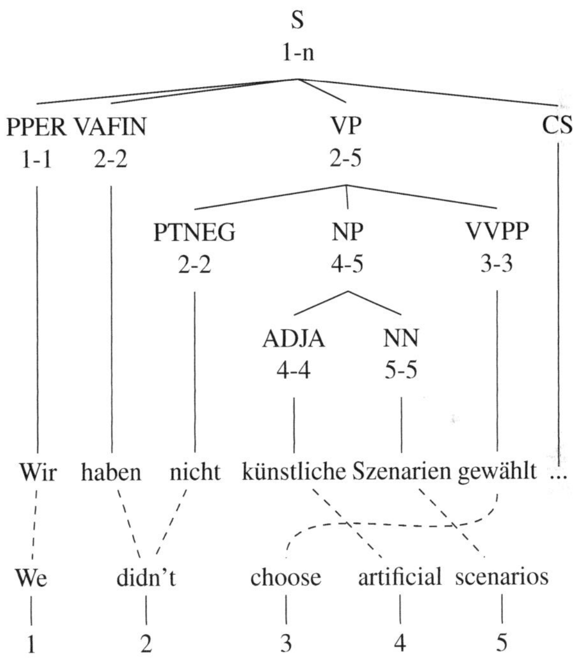

Figure 2: Example training sentence used to extract reordering rules

In a first step the reordering rule has to be found. We extract the rules from a word aligned corpus where a syntactic parse tree is provided for each source side sentence. We traverse the tree top down and scan each subtree for reorderings, i.e. crossings of alignment links between source and target sentence. If there is a reordering, we extract a rule that rearranges the source side constituents according to the order of the corresponding words on the target side. Each constituent in a subtree comprises one or more words. We determine the lowest (min) and highest (max) alignment point for each constituent c_k and thus determine the range of the constituent on the target side. This can be formalized as $min(c_k) = min\{j|f_i \in c_k; a_i = j\}$ and $max(c_k) = max\{j|f_i \in c_k; a_i = j\}$. To illustrate the process, we have annotated the parse tree in Figure 2 with the alignment points (min-max) for each constituent.

After defining the range, we check for the following conditions in order to determine whether to extract a reordering rule.

1. all constituents have a non-empty range
2. source and target word order differ

First, for each subtree at least one word in each constituent needs to be aligned. Otherwise it is not possible to determine a conclusive order. Second, we check whether there is actually a reordering, i.e. the target language words are not in the same order as the constituents in the source language: $min(c_k) > min(c_{k+1})$ and $max(c_k) > max(c_{k+1})$.

Once we find a reordering rule to extract, we calculate the probability of this rule as the relative frequency with which such a reordering occurred in all subtrees of the training corpus divided by the number of total occurrences of this subtree in the corpus. We only store rules for reorderings that occur more than 5 times in the corpus.

4.1.1 Partial Rules

The syntactic parse trees of German sentences are quite flat, i.e. a subtree usually has many children. When a rule is extracted, it always consists of the head of the subtree and all its children. The application requires that the applicable rule matches the complete subtree: the head and all its children. However, most of the time only some of the children are actually involved in a reordering. There are also many different subtree variants that are quite similar. In verb phrases or noun phrases, for example, modifiers such as prepositional phrases or adverbial phrases can be added nearly arbitrarily. In order to generalize the tree-based reordering rules, we extend the rule extraction. We do not only extract the rules from the complete child sequence, but also from any continuous child sequence in a constituent. This way, we extract generalized rules which can be applied more often. Formally, for each subtree $h \rightarrow c_1^n = c_1 c_2 ... c_n$ that matches the constraints presented in Section 4.1, we modify the basic rule extraction to: $\forall i, j 1 \leq i < j \leq n : h \rightarrow c_i^j$. It could be argued that the partial rules might be not as reliable as the specific rules. In Section 6 we will show that such generalizations are meaningful and can have a positive effect on the translation quality.

4.2 Rule Application

During the training of the system all reordering rules are extracted from the parallel corpus. Prior to translation the rules are applied to the original source text. Each rule is applied independently producing a reordering variant of that sentence. The original sentence and all reordering variants are stored in a word lattice which is later used as input to the decoder. The rules may be applied recursively to already reordered paths. If more than one rule can be applied, all paths are added to the lattice unless the rules generate the same output. In this case only the rule with the highest probability is applied.

The edges in a word lattice for one sentence are assigned transition probabilities as follows. In the monotone path with original word order all transition probabilities are initially set to 1. In a reordered path the first branching transition is assigned the probability of the rule that generated the path. All other transition probabilities in this path are set to 1. Whenever a reordered path branches from the monotone path, the probability of the branching edge is substracted from the probability of the monotone edge. However, a minimum probability of 0.05 is reserved for the monotone edge. The score of the complete path is computed as the product of the transition probabilities. During decoding the best path is searched for by including the score for the current path weighted by the weight for the reordering model in the log-linear model. In order to enable efficient decoding we limit the lattice size by only applying rules with a probability higher than a predefined threshold.

4.2.1 Recursive Rule Application

As mentioned above, the tree-based rules may be applied recursively. That means, after one rule is applied to the source sentence, a reordered path may

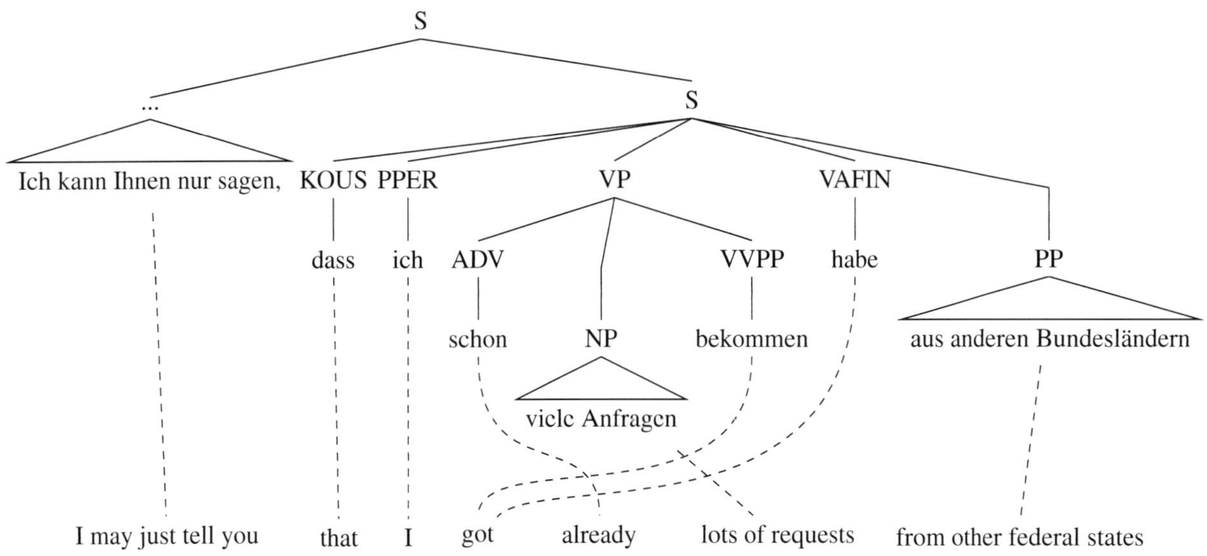

Figure 3: Example parse tree with separated verb particles

be reordered again. The reason is the structure of the syntactic parse trees. Verbs and their particles are typically not located within the same subtree. Hence, they cannot be covered by one reordering rule. A separate rule is extracted for each subtree. Figure 3 demonstrates this in an example. The two parts that belong to the verb in this German sentence, namely *bekommen* and *habe*, are not located within the same constituent. The finite verb *habe* forms a constituent of its own and the participle *bekommen* forms part of the VP constituent. In English the finite verb and the participle need to be placed next to each other. In order to rearrange the source language words according to the target language word order, the following two reordering movements need to be performed: the finite verb *habe* needs to be placed before the VP constituent and the participle *bekommen* needs to be moved within the VP constituent to the first position. Only if both movements are performed, the right word order can be generated.

However, the reordering model only considers one subtree at a time when extracting reordering rules. In this case two rules are learned, but if they are applied to the source sentence separately, they will end up in separate paths in the word lattice. The decoder then has to choose which path to translate: the one where the finite verb is placed before the VP constituent **or** the path where the participle is at the first position in the VP constituent.

To counter this drawback the rules may be applied recursively to the new paths created by our reordering rules. We use the same rules, but newly created paths are fed back into the queue of sentences to be reordered. However, we only apply the rules to parts of the reordered sentence that are still in the original word order and restrict the recursion depth.

5 Combining reordering methods

In order to get a deeper insight into their individual strengths we compare the reordering methods on different linguistic levels and also combine them to investigate whether gains can be increased. We address the word level using the lexicalized reordering, the morphosyntactic level by POS-based reordering and the constituent level by tree-based reordering.

5.1 POS-based and tree-based rules

The training of the POS-based reordering is performed as described in (Rottmann and Vogel, 2007) for short-range reordering rules, such as *VVIMP VMFIN PPER* → *PPER VMFIN VVIMP*. Long-range reordering rules trained according to (Niehues and Kolss, 2009) include gaps matching longer spans of arbitrary POS sequences (*VAFIN * VVPP* → *VAFIN VVPP **). The POS-based reordering used in our experiments always includes both short and long-range rules.

The tree-based rules are trained separately as described above. First the POS-based rules are applied to the monotone path of the source sentence and then the tree-based rules are applied independently, producing separate paths.

5.2 Rule-based and lexicalized reordering

As described in Section 4.2 we create word lattices that encode the reordering variants. The lexicalized reordering model stores for each phrase pair the probabilities for possible reordering orientations at the incoming and outgoing phrase boundaries: monotone, swap and discontinuous. In order to apply the lexicalized reordering model on lattices the original position of each word is stored in the lattice. While the translation hypothesis is generated, the reordering orientation with respect to the original position of the words is checked at each phrase boundary. The probability for the respective orientation is included as an additional score.

6 Results

The tree-based models are applied for German-English and German-French translation. Results are measured in case-sensitive BLEU (Papineni et al., 2002).

6.1 General System Description

First we describe the general system architecture which underlies all the systems used later on. We use a phrase-based decoder (Vogel, 2003) that takes word lattices as input. Optimization is performed using MERT with respect to BLEU. All POS-based or tree-based systems apply monotone translation only. Baseline systems without reordering rules use a distance-based reordering model. In addition, a lexicalized reordering model as described in (Koehn et al., 2005) is applied where indicated. POS tags and parse trees are generated using the Tree Tagger (Schmid, 1994) and the Stanford Parser (Rafferty and Manning, 2008).

6.1.1 Data

The German-English system is trained on the provided data of the WMT 2012. news-test2010 and news-test2011 are used for development and testing. The type of data used for training, development and testing the German-French system is similar to WMT data, except that 2 references are available. The training corpus for the reordering models consist of the word-aligned Europarl and News Commentary corpora where POS tags and parse trees are generated for the source side.

6.2 German-English

We built systems using POS-based and tree-based reordering and show the impact of the individual models as well as their combination on the translation quality. The results are presented in Table 1.

For each system, two different setups were evaluated. First, with a distance-based reordering model only (noLexRM) and with an additional lexicalized reordering model (LexRM). The baseline system which uses no reordering rules at all allows a reordering window of 5 in the decoder for both setups. For all systems where reordering rules are applied, monotone translation is performed. Since the rules take over the main reordering job, only monotone translation is necessary from the reordered word lattice input. In this experiment, we compare the tree-based rules with and without recursion, and the partial rules.

System / Rule Type	noLexRM		LexRM	
	Dev	Test	Dev	Test
Baseline (no Rules)	22.82	21.06	23.54	21.61
POS	24.33	21.98	24.42	22.15
Tree	24.01	21.92	24.24	22.01
Tree rec.	24.37	21.97	24.53	22.19
Tree rec.+ par.	24.31	22.21	24.65	22.27
POS + Tree	24.57	22.21	24.91	22.47
POS + Tree rec.	24.61	22.39	24.81	22.45
POS + Tree rec.+ par.	24.80	22.45	24.78	22.70

Table 1: *German-English*

Compared to the baseline system using distance-based reordering only, 1.4 BLEU points can be gained by applying combined POS and tree-based reordering. The tree rules including partial rules and recursive application alone achieve already a better performance than the POS rules, but using them all in combination leads to an improvement of 0.4 BLEU points over the POS-based reordering alone. When lexicalized reordering is added, the relative improvements are similar: 1.1 BLEU points compared to the Baseline and 0.55 BLEU points over the POS-based reordering. We can therefore argue that the individual rule types as well as the lexicalized reordering model seem to address complementary reordering issues and can be combined successfully to obtain an even better translation quality.

We applied only tree rules with a probability of 0.1 and higher. Partial rules require a threshold of 0.4 to be applied, since they are less reliable. In order to prevent the lattices from growing too large, the recursive rule application is restricted to a maximum recursion depth of 3. These values were set according to the results of preliminary experiments investigating the impact of the rule probabilities on the translation quality. Normal rules and partial rules are not mixed during recursive application.

With the best system we performed a final experiment on the official testset of the WMT 2012 and achieved a score of 23.73 which is 0.4 BLEU points better than the best constrained submission.

6.3 Translation Examples

Example 2 shows how the translation of the sentence presented above is improved by adding the tree-based rules. We can see that using tree constituents in the reordering model indeed addresses the problem of verb particles and especially missing verb parts in German.

Example 2:

Src: ..., *nachdem ich eine Weile im Internet gesucht habe.*

Gloss: ..., *after I a while in-the Internet searched have.*

POS: ... *as I have for some time on the Internet.*

+Tree: ... *after I have looked for a while on the Internet.*

Example 3 shows another aspect of how the tree-based rules work. With the help of the tree-based reordering rules, it is possible to relocate the separated prefix of German verbs and find the correct translation. The verb *vorschlagen* consist of the main verb (MV) *schlagen* (here conjugated as *schlägt*) and the prefix (PX) *vor*. Depending on the verb form and sentence type, the prefix must be separated from the main verb and is located in a different part of the sentence. The two parts of the verb can also have individual meanings. Although the translation of the verb stem were correct if it were the full verb, not recognizing the separated prefix and ignoring it in translation, corrupts the meaning of the sentence. With the help of the tree-based rules, the dependency between the main verb and its prefix is resolved and the correct translation can be chosen.

6.4 German-French

The same experiments were tested on German-French translation. For this language pair, similar improvements could be achieved by combining POS and tree-based reordering rules and applying a lexicalized reordering model in addition. Table 2 shows the results. Up to 0.7 BLEU points could be gained by adding tree rules and another 0.1 by lexicalized reordering.

Rule Type \ System	noLexRM		LexRM	
	Dev	Test	Dev	Test
POS	41.29	38.07	42.04	38.55
POS + Tree	41.94	38.47	42.44	38.57
POS + Tree rec.	42.35	38.66	42.80	38.71
POS + Tree rec.+ par.	42.48	38.79	42.87	38.88

Table 2: *German-French*

6.5 Binarized Syntactic Trees

Even though related work using syntactic parse trees in SMT for reordering purposes (Jiang et al., 2010) have reported an advantage of binarized parse trees over standard parse trees, our model did not benefit from binarized parse trees. It seems that the flat hierarchical structure of standard parse trees enables our reordering model to learn the order of the constituents most efficiently.

7 Human Evaluation

7.1 Sentence-based comparison

In order to have an additional perspective of the impact of our tree-based reordering, we also provide a human evaluation of the translation output of the German-English system without the lexicalized reordering model. 250 translation hypotheses were selected to be annotated. For each input sentence two translations generated by different systems were presented, one applying POS-based reordering only and the other one applying both POS-based and tree-based reordering rules. The hypotheses were anonymized and presented in random order.

Table 3 shows the BLEU scores of the analyzed systems and the manual judgement of comparative, subjective translation quality. In 50.8% of the sen-

Example 3:
Src: *Die RPG Byty schlägt ihnen in den Schreiben eine Mieterhöhung von ca. 15 bis 38 Prozent vor.*
Gloss: *The RPG Byty proposes-MV them in the letters a rent increase of ca. 15 to 38 percent proposes-PX*
POS: *The RPG Byty beats them in the letter, a rental increase of around 15 to 38 percent.*
+Tree: *The RPG Byty proposes them in the letters a rental increase of around 15 to 38 percent.*

System	BLEU	wins	%
POS Rules	21.98	58	23.2
POS + Tree Rules rec. par.	22.45	127	50.8

Table 3: *Human Evaluation of Translation quality*

Type	all	exist	position	form
Improvements	48	22	21	5
Degradations	16	2	11	3

Table 4: *Manual Analysis of verbs*

tences, the translation generated by the system using tree-based rules was judged to be better, whereas in 23.2% of the cases the system without tree-based rules was rated better. For 26% of the sentences the translation quality was very similar. Consequently, in 76.8% of the cases the tree-based system produced a translation that is either better or of the same quality as the system using POS rules only.

7.2 Analysis of verbs

Since the verbs in German-to-English translation were one of the issues that the tree-based reordering model should address, a more detailed analysis was performed on the first 165 sentences. We especially investigated the changes regarding the verbs between the translations stemming from the system using the POS-based reordering only and the one using both the POS and the tree-based model. We examined three aspects of the verbs in the two translations. Each change introduced by the tree-based reordering model was first classified either as an improvement or a degradation of the translation quality. Secondly, it was assigned to one of the following categories: **exist**, **position** or **form**. In case of an improvement, **exist** means a verb existed in the translation due to the tree-based model, which did not exist before. A degradation in this category means that a verb was removed from the translation when including the tree-based reordering model. An improvement or degradation in the category **position** or **form** means that the verb position or verb form was improved or degraded, respectively.

Table 4 shows the results of this analysis. In total, 48 of the verb changes were identified as improvements, while only 16 were regarded as degradations of translation quality. Improvements mainly concern improved verb position in the sentence and verbs that could be translated with the help of the tree-based rules that were not there before. Even though also degradations were introduced by the tree-based reordering model, the improvements outweigh them.

8 Conclusion

We have presented a reordering method based on syntactic tree constituents to model long-range reorderings in SMT more reliably. Furthermore, we combined the reordering methods addressing different linguistic abstraction levels. Experiments on German-English and German-French translation showed that the best translation quality could be achieved by combining POS-based and tree-based rules. Adding a lexicalized reordering model increased the translation quality even further. In total we could reach up to 0.7 BLEU points of improvement by adding tree-based and lexicalized reordering compared to only POS-based rules. Up to 1.1 BLEU points were gained over to a baseline system using a lexicalized reordering model.

A human evaluation showed a preference of the POS+Tree-based reordering method in most cases. A detailed analysis of the verbs in the translation outputs revealed that the tree-based reordering model indeed addresses verb constructions and improves the translation of German verbs.

Acknowledgments

This work was partly achieved as part of the Quaero Programme, funded by OSEO, French State agency for innovation. The research leading to these results has received funding from the European Union Seventh Framework Programme (FP7/2007-2013) under grant agreement n° 287658.

References

David Chiang. 2005. A hierarchical phrase-based model for statistical machine translation. In *Proceedings of the 43rd Annual Meeting on Association for Computational Linguistics*, ACL '05, pages 263–270, Stroudsburg, PA, USA.

Michael Collins, Philipp Koehn, and Ivona Kučerová. 2005. Clause Restructuring for Statistical Machine Translation. In *Proceedings of ACL 2005*, Ann Arbor, Michigan.

Marta R. Costa-jussà and José A. R. Fonollosa. 2006. Statistical Machine Reordering. In *Conference on Empirical Methods on Natural Language Processing (EMNLP 2006)*, Sydney, Australia.

Josep M. Crego and Nizar Habash. 2008. Using Shallow Syntax Information to Improve Word Alignment and Reordering for SMT. In *ACL-HLT 2008*, Columbus, Ohio, USA.

John DeNero and Jakob Uszkoreit. 2011. Inducing sentence structure from parallel corpora for reordering. In *Proceedings of EMNLP 2011*, pages 193–203, Edinburgh, Scotland, UK.

Dmitriy Genzel. 2010. Automatically learning source-side reordering rules for large scale machine translation. In *Proceedings of COLING 2010*, Beijing, China.

Nizar Habash. 2007. Syntactic preprocessing for statistical machine translation. *Proceedings of the 11th MT Summit.*

Jie Jiang, Jinhua Du, and Andy Way. 2010. Improved phrase-based smt with syntactic reordering patterns learned from lattice scoring. In *Proceedings of AMTA 2010*, Denver, CO, USA.

M. Khalilov, J.A.R. Fonollosa, and M. Dras. 2009. A new subtree-transfer approach to syntax-based reordering for statistical machine translation. In *Proc. of the 13th Annual Conference of the European Association for Machine Translation (EAMT'09)*, pages 198–204, Barcelona, Spain.

Philipp Koehn, Amittai Axelrod, Alexandra Birch Mayne, Chris Callison-Burch, Miles Osborne, and David Talbot. 2005. Edinburgh system description for the 2005 iwslt speech translation evaluation. In *International Workshop on Spoken Language Translation.*

Philipp Koehn, Hieu Hoang, Alexandra Birch, Chris Callison-Burch, Marcello Federico, Nicola Bertoldi, Brooke Cowan, Wade Shen, Christine Moran, Richard Zens, et al. 2007. Moses: Open source toolkit for statistical machine translation. In *Annual meeting-association for computational linguistics*, volume 45, page 2.

Jan Niehues and Muntsin Kolss. 2009. A POS-Based Model for Long-Range Reorderings in SMT. In *Fourth Workshop on Statistical Machine Translation (WMT 2009)*, Athens, Greece.

Kishore Papineni, Salim Roukos, Todd Ward, and Wei-Jing Zhu. 2002. Bleu: a Method for Automatic Evaluation of Machine Translation. Technical Report RC22176 (W0109-022), IBM Research Division, T. J. Watson Research Center.

Maja Popović and Hermann Ney. 2006. POS-based Word Reorderings for Statistical Machine Translation. In *International Conference on Language Resources and Evaluation (LREC 2006)*, Genoa, Italy.

Anna N. Rafferty and Christopher D. Manning. 2008. Parsing three German treebanks: lexicalized and unlexicalized baselines. In *Proceedings of the Workshop on Parsing German*, Columbus, Ohio.

Kay Rottmann and Stephan Vogel. 2007. Word Reordering in Statistical Machine Translation with a POS-Based Distortion Model. In *TMI*, Skövde, Sweden.

Helmut Schmid. 1994. Probabilistic Part-of-Speech Tagging Using Decision Trees. In *International Conference on New Methods in Language Processing*, Manchester, UK.

Christoph Tillmann. 2004. A unigram orientation model for statistical machine translation. In *Proceedings of HLT-NAACL 2004: Short Papers*, pages 101–104.

Stephan Vogel. 2003. SMT Decoder Dissected: Word Reordering. In *Int. Conf. on Natural Language Processing and Knowledge Engineering*, Beijing, China.

Chao Wang, Michael Collins, and Philipp Koehn. 2007. Chinese syntactic reordering for statistical machine translation. In *Proceedings of the 2007 Joint Conference on Empirical Methods in Natural Language Processing and Computational Natural Language Learning (EMNLP-CoNLL)*, pages 737–745.

Fei Xia and Michael McCord. 2004. Improving a statistical mt system with automatically learned rewrite patterns. In *Proceedings of COLING 2004*, Geneva, Switzerland.

Kenji Yamada and Kevin Knight. 2001. A syntax-based statistical translation model. In *Proceedings of the 39th Annual Meeting on Association for Computational Linguistics*, ACL '01, pages 523–530, Stroudsburg, PA, USA.

Yuqi Zhang, Richard Zens, and Hermann Ney. 2007. Chunk-Level Reordering of Source Language Sentences with Automatically Learned Rules for Statistical Machine Translation. In *HLT-NAACL Workshop on Syntax and Structure in Statistical Translation*, Rochester, NY, USA.

Andreas Zollmann and Ashish Venugopal. 2006. Syntax augmented machine translation via chart parsing. In *Proceedings of the Workshop on Statistical Machine Translation*, StatMT '06, pages 138–141, Stroudsburg, PA, USA.

Combining Top-down and Bottom-up Search for Unsupervised Induction of Transduction Grammars

Markus SAERS and **Karteek ADDANKI** and **Dekai WU**
Human Language Technology Center
Dept. of Computer Science and Engineering
Hong Kong University of Science and Technology
{masaers|vskaddanki|dekai}@cs.ust.hk

Abstract

We show that combining *both* bottom-up rule chunking and top-down rule segmentation search strategies in purely unsupervised learning of phrasal inversion transduction grammars yields significantly better translation accuracy than either strategy alone. Previous approaches have relied on incrementally building larger rules by chunking smaller rules bottom-up; we introduce a complementary top-down model that incrementally builds shorter rules by segmenting larger rules. Specifically, we combine iteratively chunked rules from Saers *et al.* (2012) with our new iteratively segmented rules. These integrate seamlessly because both stay strictly within a pure transduction grammar framework inducing under matching models during both training and testing—instead of decoding under a completely different model architecture than what is assumed during the training phases, which violates an elementary principle of machine learning and statistics. To be able to drive induction top-down, we introduce a minimum description length objective that trades off maximum likelihood against model size. We show empirically that combining the more liberal rule chunking model with a more conservative rule segmentation model results in significantly better translations than either strategy in isolation.

1 Introduction

In this paper we combine both bottom-up chunking and top-down segmentation as search directions in the unsupervised pursuit of an inversion transduction grammar (ITG); we also show that the combination of the resulting grammars is superior to either of them in isolation. For the bottom-up chunking approach we use the method reported in Saers *et al.* (2012), and for the top-down segmentation approach, we introduce a minimum description length (MDL) learning objective. The new learning objective is similar to the Bayesian maximum a posteriori objective, and makes it possible to learn top-down, which is impossible using maximum likelihood, as the initial grammar that rewrites the start symbol to all sentence pairs in the training data already maximizes the likelihood of the training data. Since both approaches result in stochastic ITGs, they can be easily combined into a single stochastic ITG which allows for seamless combination. The point of our present work is that the two different search strategies result in very different grammars so that the combination of them is superior in terms of translation accuracy to either of them in isolation.

The transduction grammar approach has the advantage that induction, tuning and testing are optimized on the exact same underlying model—this used to be a given in machine learning and statistical prediction, but has been largely ignored in the statistical machine translation (SMT) community, where most current SMT approaches to learning phrase translations that (a) require enormous amounts of run-time memory, and (b) contain a high degree of redundancy. In particular, phrase-based SMT models such as Koehn *et al.* (2003) and Chiang (2007) often search for candidate translation segments and transduction rules by committing to a word alignment that is completely alien to the grammar, as it is learned with very different models (Brown *et al.* (1993), Vogel *et al.* (1996)), whose output is then combined heuristically to form the alignment actually used to extract lexical segment translations (Och and Ney, 2003). The fact that it is even possible to improve the performance of a phrase-based direct translation system by tossing away most of the learned segmental translations (Johnson *et al.*, 2007) illustrates the above points well.

Transduction grammars can also be induced from treebanks instead of unannotated corpora, which cuts down the vast search space by enforcing additional, external constraints. This approach was pioneered by Galley *et al.* (2006), and there has been a lot of research since, usually referred to as **tree-to-tree**, **tree-to-string** and **string-to-tree**, depending on where the analyses are found in the training data. This complicates the learning process by adding external constraints that are bound to match the translation model poorly; grammarians of English should not be expected to care about its relationship to Chinese. It does, however, constitute a way to borrow nonterminal categories that help the translation model.

It is also possible for the word alignments leading to phrase-based SMT models to be learned through transduction grammars (see for example Cherry and Lin (2007), Zhang *et al.* (2008), Blunsom *et al.* (2008), Saers and Wu (2009), Haghighi *et al.* (2009), Blunsom *et al.* (2009), Saers *et al.* (2010), Blunsom and Cohn (2010), Saers and Wu (2011), Neubig *et al.* (2011), Neubig *et al.* (2012)). Even when the SMT model is hierarchical, most of the information encoded in the grammar is tossed away, when the learned model is reduced to a word alignment. A word alignment can only encode the lexical relationships that exist between a sentence pair according to a single parse tree, which means that the rest of the model: the alternative parses and the syntactic structure, is ignored.

The minimum description length (MDL) objective that we will be using to drive the learning will provide a way to escape the maximum-likelihood-of-the-data-given-the-model optimum that we start out with. However, going only by MDL will also lead to a degenerate case, where the size of the grammar is allowed to shrink regardless of how unlikely the corpus becomes. Instead, we will balance the length of the grammar with the probability of the corpus given the grammar. This has a natural Bayesian interpretation where the length of the grammar acts as a prior over the structure of the grammar.

Similar approaches have been used before, but to induce monolingual grammars. Stolcke and Omohundro (1994) use a method similar to MDL called *Bayesian model merging* to learn the structure of hidden Markov models as well as stochastic context-free grammars. The SCFGs are induced by allowing sequences of nonterminals to be replaced with a single nonterminal (chunking) as well as allowing two nonterminals to merge into one. Grünwald (1996) uses it to learn nonterminal categories in a context-free grammar. It has also been used to interpret visual scenes by classifying the activity that goes on in a video sequences (Si *et al.*, 2011). Our work in this paper is markedly different to even the previous NLP work in that (a) we induce an inversion transduction grammar (Wu, 1997) rather than a monolingual grammar, and (b) we focus on learning the terminal segments rather than the nonterminal categories.

The similar Bayesian approaches to finding the model structure of ITGs have been tried before, but only to generate alignments that mismatched translation models are then trained on, rather than using the ITG directly as translation model, which we do. Zhang *et al.* (2008) use variational Bayes with a sparsity prior over the parameters to prevent the size of the grammar to explode when allowing for adjacent terminals in the Viterbi biparses to chunk together. Blunsom *et al.* (2008), Blunsom *et al.* (2009) and Blunsom and Cohn (2010) use Gibbs sampling to find good phrasal translations. Neubig *et al.* (2011) and Neubig *et al.* (2012) use a method more similar to ours, but with a Pitman-Yor process as prior over the structures.

The idea of iteratively segmenting the existing sentence pairs to find good phrasal translations has also been tried before; Vilar and Vidal (2005) introduces the Recursive Alignment Model, which recursively determines whether a bispan is a good enough translation on its own (using IBM model 1), or if it should be split into two bispans (either in straight or inverted order). The model uses length of the input sentence to determine whether to split or not, and uses very limited local information about the split point to determine where to split. Training the parameters is done with a maximum likelihood objective. In contrast, our model is one single generative model (as opposed to an *ad hoc* model), trained with a minimum description length objective (rather than trying to maximize the probability of the training data).

The rest of the paper is structured so that we first take a closer look at the minimum description length principle that will be used to drive the top-down search (Section 2). We then show how the top-down grammar is learned (Sections 3 and 4), before showing how we combine the new grammar with that of Saers *et al.* (2012) (Section 5). We then detail the experimental setup that will substantiate our claims empirically (Section 6) before interpreting the results of those experiments (Section 7). Finally, we offer some conclusions (Section 8).

2 Minimum description length

The minimum description length principle is about finding the optimal balance between the size of a model and the size of some data given the model (Solomonoff (1959), Rissanen (1983)). Consider the information theoretical problem of encoding some data with a model, and then sending both the encoded data *and* the information needed to decode the data (the model) over a channel; the minimum description length would be the minimum number of bits sent over the channel. The encoded data can be interpreted as carrying the information necessary to disambiguate the ambiguities or uncertainties that the model has about the data. Theoretically, the model can *grow in size* and become *more certain* about the data, and it can *shrink in size* and become *more uncertain* about the data. An intuitive interpretation of this is that the exceptions, which are a part of the encoded data, can be moved into the model itself. By doing so, the size of the model increases, but there is no longer an exception that needs to be conveyed about the data. Some "exceptions" occur frequently enough that it is a good idea to incorporate them into the model, and some do not; finding the optimal balance minimizes the total description length.

Formally, the description length (DL) is:

$$\mathrm{DL}\left(M,D\right)=\mathrm{DL}\left(D|M\right)+\mathrm{DL}\left(M\right) \quad (1)$$

Where M is the model and D is the data. Note the clear parallel to probabilities that have been moved into the logarithmic domain.

In natural language processing, we never have complete data to train on, so we need our models to generalize to unseen data. A model that is very certain about the training data runs the risk of not being able to generalize to new data: it is over-fitting. It is bad enough when estimating the parameters of a transduction grammar, and catastrophic when inducing the structure of the grammar. The key concept that we want to capture when learning the structure of a transduction grammar is *generalization*. This is the property that allow it to translate new, unseen, input. The challenge is to pin down what generalization actually is, and how to measure it.

One property of generalization for grammars is that it will lower the probability of the training data. This may seem counterintuitive, but can be understood as moving some of the probability mass away from the training data and putting it in unseen data. A second property is that rules that are specific to the training data can be eliminated from the grammar (or replaced with less specific rules that generate the same thing). The second property would shorten the description of the grammar, and the first would make the description of the corpus given the grammar longer. That is: generalization raises the first term and lowers the second in Equation 1. A good generalization will lower the total MDL, whereas a poor one will raise it; a good generalization will trade a little data *certainty* for more model *parsimony*.

2.1 Measuring the length of a corpus

The information-theoretic view of the problem also gives a hint at the operationalization of *length*. Shannon (1948) stipulates that the number of bits it takes to encode that a probabilistic variable has taken a certain value can be encoded using as little as the negative logarithmic probability of that outcome.

Following this, the parallel corpus given the transduction grammar gives the number of bits required to encode it: $\mathrm{DL}\left(C|G\right)=-\log_2\left(P\left(C|G\right)\right)$, where C is the corpus and G is the grammar.

2.2 Measuring the length of an ITG

Since information theory deals with encoding sequences of symbols, we need some way to serialize an inversion transduction grammar (ITG) into a message whose length can be measured.

To serialize an ITG, we first need to determine the alphabet that the message will be written in. We need one symbol for every nonterminal, L_0-terminal and L_1-terminal. We will also make the assumption that all these symbols are used in at least one rule, so that it is sufficient to serialize the rules in order to express the entire grammar. To serialize the rules, we need some kind of delimiter to know where one rule starts and the next ends; we will exploit the fact that we also need to specify whether the rule is straight or inverted (unary rules are assumed to be straight), and merge these two functions into one symbol. This gives the union of the symbols of the grammar and the set $\{[], \langle\rangle\}$, where $[]$ signals the beginning of a straight rule, and $\langle\rangle$ signals the beginning of an inverted rule. The serialized format of a rule will be: rule type/start marker, followed by the left-hand side nonterminal, followed by all right-hand side symbols. The symbols on the right-hand sides are either nonterminals or **biterminals**—pairs of L_0-terminals and L_1-terminals that model translation equivalences. The serialized form of a grammar is the serialized form of all rules concatenated.

Consider the following toy grammar:

$$S \to A, \qquad A \to \langle AA \rangle, \quad A \to [AA],$$
$$A \to \text{have}/\bullet \;\; ; \;\; A \to \text{yes}/\bullet \;\; ; \;\; A \to \text{yes}/\bullet \;\; \bullet$$

Its serialized form would be:

$$[]SA\langle\rangle AAA[]AAA[]A\text{have}\bullet \;\; []A\text{yes}\bullet \;\; []A\text{yes}\bullet \;\; \bullet$$

Now we can, again turn to information theory to arrive at an encoding for this message. Assuming a uniform distribution over the symbols, each symbol will require $-\log_2\left(\frac{1}{N}\right)$ bits to encode (where N is the number of different symbols—the type count). The above example has 8 symbols, meaning that each symbol requires 3 bits. The entire message is 23 symbols long, which means that we need 69 bits to encode it.

3 Model initialization

Rather than starting out with a general transduction grammar and fitting it to the training data, we do the exact opposite: we start with a transduction grammar that fits the training data as well as possible, and generalize from there. The transduction grammar that fits the training data the best is the one where the start symbol rewrites to the full sentence pairs that it has to generate. It is also possible to add any number of nonterminal symbols in the layer between the start symbol and the bisentences without altering the probability of the training data. We take advantage of this by allowing for one intermediate symbol so that the start symbol conforms to the normal form and always rewrites to precisely one nonterminal symbol. This violate the MDL principle, as the introduction of new symbols, by definition, makes the description of the model longer, but conforming to the normal form of ITGs was deemed more important than strictly minimizing the description length. Our initial grammar thus looks like this:

$$\begin{aligned}
S &\to A, \\
A &\to e_{0..T_0}/f_{0..V_0}, \\
A &\to e_{0..T_1}/f_{0..V_1}, \\
&\ldots, \\
A &\to e_{0..T_N}/f_{0..V_N}
\end{aligned}$$

Where S is the start symbol, A is the nonterminal, N is the number of sentence pairs in the training corpus, T_i is the length of the ith output sentence (which makes $e_{0..T_i}$ the ith output sentence), and V_i is the length of the ith input sentence (which makes $f_{0..V_i}$ the ith input sentence).

4 Model generalization

To generalize the initial inversion transduction grammar we need to identify parts of the existing biterminals that could be validly used in isolation, and allow them to combine with other segments. This is the very feature that allows a finite transduction grammar to generate an infinite set of sentence pairs. Doing this moves some of the probability mass, which was concentrated in the training data, to unseen data—the very definition of generalization. Our general strategy is to propose a number of sets of biterminal rules and a place to segment them, evaluate how the description length would change if we were to apply one of these sets of segmentations to the grammar, and commit to the best set. That is: we do a greedy search over the power set of possible segmentations of the rule set. As we will see, this intractable problem can be reasonable efficiently approximated, which is what we have implemented and tested.

The key component in the approach is the ability to evaluate how the description length would change if a specific segmentation was made in the grammar.

This can then be extended to a set of segmentations, which only leaves the problem of generating suitable sets of segmentations.

The key to a successful segmentation is to maximize the potential for reuse. Any segment that can be reused saves model size. Consider the terminal rule:

$A \rightarrow$ five thousand yen is my limit/
• • • • • • • • • • • • • • • • • • • •

(Chinese gloss: 'wǒ zùi dūo chū wǔ qīan rì yúan'). This rule can be split into three rules:

$A \rightarrow \langle AA \rangle,$
$A \rightarrow$ five thousand yen/• • • • ; • • •
$A \rightarrow$ is my limit/• • • • • • • •

Note that the original rule consists of 16 symbols (in our encoding scheme), whereas the new three rules consists of $4 + 9 + 9 = 22$ symbols. It is reasonable to believe that the bracketing inverted rule is in the grammar already, but this still leaves 18 symbols, which is decidedly longer than 16 symbols—and we need to get the length to be shorter if we want to see a net gain, since the length of the corpus given the grammar is likely to be longer with the segmented rules. What we really need to do is find a way to reuse the lexical rules that came out of the segmentation. Now suppose the grammar also contained this terminal rule:

$A \rightarrow$ the total fare is five thousand yen/
• •

(Chinese gloss: 'zǒng gòng de fèi yòng shì wǔ qīan rì yúan'). This rule can also be split into three rules:

$A \rightarrow [AA],$
$A \rightarrow$ the total fare is/• • • • • • ; • • • •
$A \rightarrow$ five thousand yen/• • • • • • • •

Again, we will assume that the structural rule is already present in the grammar, the old rule was 19 symbols long, and the two new terminal rules are $12+9 = 21$ symbols long. Again we are out of luck, as the new rules are longer than the old one, and three rules are likely to be less probable than one rule during parsing. The way to make this work is to realize that the two existing rules share a bilingual affix—a **biaffix**: "five thousand dollars" translating into "• • • • • •". If we make the two changes at the same time, we get rid of $16 + 19 = 35$ symbols worth of rules, and introduce a mere $9 + 9 + 12 = 30$ symbols worth of rules (assuming the structural rules are already in the grammar). Making these two changes at the same time is essential, as the length of the five saved symbols can be used to offset the likely increase in the length of the corpus given the data. And of course: the more rules we can find with shared biaffixes, the more likely we are to find a good set of segmentations.

Our algorithm takes advantage of the above observation by focusing on the biaffixes found in the training data. Each biaffix defines a set of lexical rules paired up with a possible segmentation. We evaluate the biaffixes by estimating the change in description length associated with committing to all the segmentations defined by a biaffix. This allows us to find the best set of segmentations, but rather than committing only to the one best set of segmentations, we will collect all sets which would improve description length, and try to commit to as many of them as possible. The pseudocode for our algorithm is as follows:

```
G                      // The grammar
biaffixes_to_rules     // Maps biaffixes to the
                       //    rules they occur in
biaffixes_delta = []   // A list of biaffixes and
                       //    their DL impact on G
for each biaffix b :
   delta = eval_dl(b, biaffixes_to_rules[b], G)
   if (delta < 0)
      biaffixes_delta.push(b, delta)
sort_by_delta(biaffixes_delta)
for each b:delta pair in biaffixes_delta :
   real_delta = eval_dl(b, biaffixes_to_rules[b], G)
   if (real_delta < 0)
      G = make_segmentations(b, biaffixes_to_rules[b], G)
```

The methods `eval_dl`, `sort_by_delta` and `make_segmentations` evaluates the impact on description length that committing to a biaffix would cause, sorts a list of biaffixes according to this delta, and applies all the changes associated with a biaffix to the grammar, respectively.

Evaluating the impact on description length breaks down into two parts: the difference in description length of the grammar $\mathrm{DL}(G') - \mathrm{DL}(G)$ (where G' is the grammar that results from applying all the changes that committing to a biaffix dictates), and the difference in description length of the corpus given the grammar $\mathrm{DL}(C|G') - \mathrm{DL}(C|G)$. These two quantities are simply added up to get the total change in description length.

The difference in grammar length is calculated as described in Section 2.2. The difference in description length of the corpus given the grammar can be calculated by biparsing the corpus, since $\mathrm{DL}(C|G') = -\log_2(P(C|p'))$ and $\mathrm{DL}(C|G) = -\log_2(P(C|p))$ where p' and p are the rule probability functions of G' and G respectively. Biparsing is, however, a very costly process that we do not want to have inside a loop. Instead, we assume that we have the original corpus probability (through biparsing *outside* the loop), and estimate the new corpus probability from it (in closed form). Given that we are splitting the rule r_0 into the three rules r_1, r_2 and r_3, and that the probability mass of r_0 is distributed uniformly over the new rules, the new rule probability function p' will be identical to p, except that:

$$\begin{aligned} p'(r_0) &= 0, \\ p'(r_1) &= p(r_1) + \frac{1}{3}p(r_0), \\ p'(r_2) &= p(r_2) + \frac{1}{3}p(r_0), \\ p'(r_3) &= p(r_3) + \frac{1}{3}p(r_0) \end{aligned}$$

Since we have eliminated all the occurrences of r_0 and replaced them with combinations of r_1, r_2 and r_3, the probability of the corpus given this new rule probability function will be:

$$P(C|p') = P(C|p)\,\frac{p'(r_1)\,p'(r_2)\,p'(r_3)}{p(r_0)}$$

To make this into a description length, we need to take the negative logarithm of the above, which results in:

$$\mathrm{DL}(C|G') = \mathrm{DL}(C|G) - \log_2\left(\frac{p'(r_1)\,p'(r_2)\,p'(r_3)}{p(r_0)}\right)$$

The difference in description length of the corpus given the grammar can now be expressed as:

$$\mathrm{DL}(C|G') - \mathrm{DL}(C|G) = -\log_2\left(\frac{p'(r_1)p'(r_2)p'(r_3)}{p(r_0)}\right)$$

To calculate the impact of a set of segmentations, we need to take all the changes into account in one go. We do this in a two-pass fashion, first calculating the new probability function (p') and the change in grammar description length (taking care not to count the same rule twice), and then, in the second pass, calculating the change in corpus description length.

5 Model combination

The model we learn by iteratively subsegmenting the training data is guaranteed to be parsimonious while retaining a decent fit to the training data; these are desirable qualities, but there is a real risk that we failed to make some generalization that we should have made; to counter this risk, we can use a model trained under more liberal conditions. We chose the approach taken by Saers *et al.* (2012) for two reasons: (a) the model has the same form as our model, which means that we can integrate it seamlessly, and (b) their aims are similar to ours but their method differs significantly; specifically, they let the model grow in size as long as the data reduces in size. Both these qualities make it a suitable complement for our model.

Assuming we have two grammars (G_a and G_b) that we want to combine, the interpolation parameter α will determine the probability function of the combined grammar such that:

$$p_{a+b}(r) = \alpha p_a(r) + (1-\alpha)p_b(r)$$

for all rules r in the union of the two rule sets, and where p_{a+b} is the rule probability function of the combined grammar and p_a and p_b are the rule probability functions of G_a and G_b respectively. Some initial experiments indicated that an α value of about 0.4 was reasonable (when G_a was the grammar obtained through the training scheme outlined above, and G_b was the grammar obtained through the training scheme outlined in Saers *et al.* (2012)), so we used 0.4 in this paper.

6 Experimental setup

We have made the claim that iterative top-down segmentation guided by the objective of minimizing the description length gives a better precision grammar than iterative bottom-up chunking, and that the combination of the two gives superior results to either

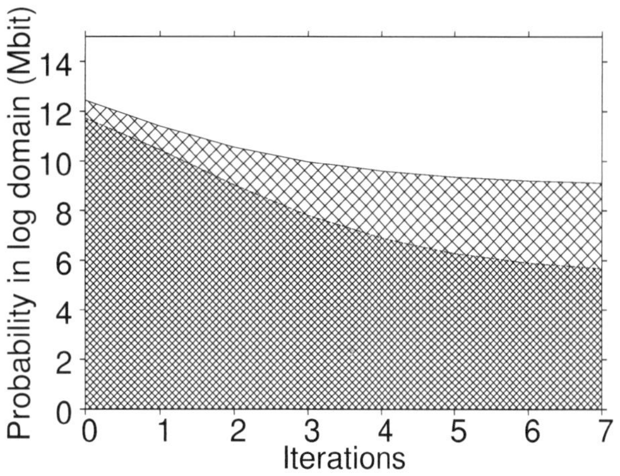

Figure 1: Description length in bits over the different iterations of top-down search. The lower portion represents DL (G) and the upper portion represents DL $(C|G)$.

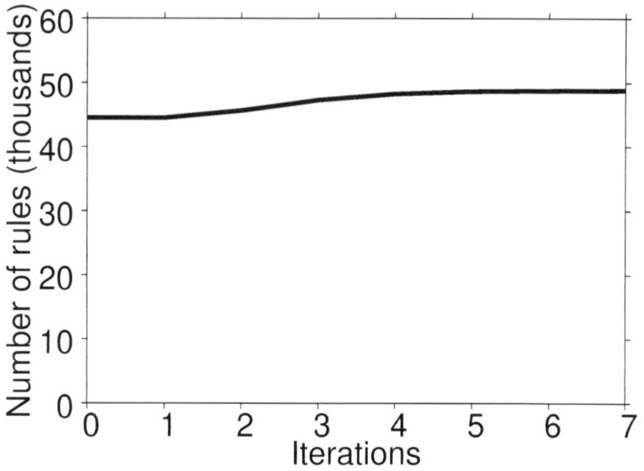

Figure 2: Number of rules learned during top-down search over the different iterations.

approach in isolation. We have outlined how this can be done in practice, and we now substantiate that claim empirically.

We will initialize a stochastic bracketing inversion transduction grammar (BITG) to rewrite it's one nonterminal symbol directly into all the sentence pairs of the training data (iteration 0). We will then segment the grammar iteratively a total of seven times (iterations 1–7). For each iteration we will record the change in description length and test the grammar. Each iteration requires us to biparse the training data, which we do with the cubic time algorithm described in Saers *et al.* (2009), with a beam width of 100.

As training data, we use the IWSLT07 Chinese–English data set (Fordyce, 2007), which contains 46,867 sentence pairs of training data, 506 Chinese sentences of development data with 16 English reference translations, and 489 Chinese sentences with 6 English reference translations each as test data; all the sentences are taken from the traveling domain. Since the Chinese is written without whitespace, we use a tool that tries to clump characters together into more "word like" sequences (Wu, 1999).

As the bottom-up grammar, we will reuse the grammar learned in Saers *et al.* (2012), specifically, we will use the BITG that was bootstrapped from a bracketing finite-state transduction grammar (BFSTG) that has been chunked twice, giving biterminals where the monolingual segments are 0–4 tokens long. The bottom-up grammar is trained on the same data as our model.

To test the learned grammars as translation models, we first tune the grammar parameters to the training data using expectation maximization (Dempster *et al.*, 1977) and parse forests acquired with the above mentioned biparser, again with a beam width of 100. To do the actual decoding, we use our in-house ITG decoder. The decoder uses a CKY-style parsing algorithm (Cocke, 1969; Kasami, 1965; Younger, 1967) and cube pruning (Chiang, 2007) to integrate the language model scores. The decoder builds an efficient hypergraph structure which is then scored using both the induced grammar and the language model. The weights for the language model and the grammar, are tuned towards BLEU (Papineni *et al.*, 2002) using MERT (Och, 2003). We use the ZMERT (Zaidan, 2009) implementation of MERT as it is a robust and flexible implementation of MERT, while being loosely coupled with the decoder. We use SRILM (Stolcke, 2002) for training a trigram language model on the English side of the training data. To evaluate the quality of the resulting translations, we use BLEU, and NIST (Doddington, 2002).

7 Experimental results

The results from running the experiments detailed in the previous section can be summarized in four graphs. Figures 1 and 2 show the size of our new, segmenting model during induction, in terms of description length and in terms of rule count. The initial ITG is at iteration 0, where the vast majority

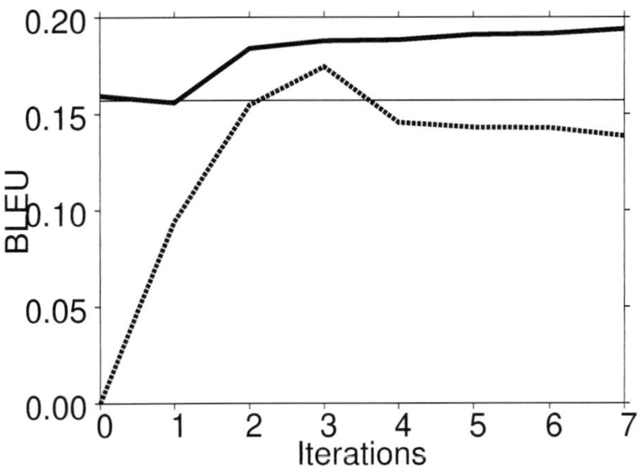

Figure 3: Variations in BLEU score over different iterations. The thin line represents the baseline bottom-up search (Saers *et al.*, 2012), the dotted line represents the top-down search, and the thick line represents the combined results.

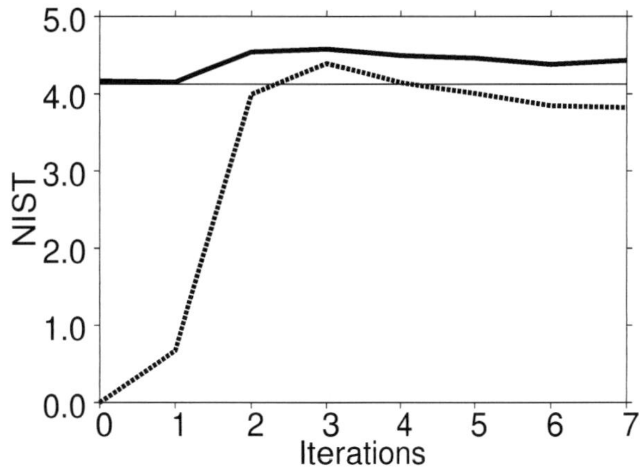

Figure 4: Variations in NIST score over different iterations. The thin line represents the baseline bottom-up search (Saers *et al.*, 2012), the dotted line represents the top-down search, and the thick line represents the combined results.

of the size is taken up by the model (DL (G)), and very little by the data (DL $(C|G)$)—just as we predicted. The trend over the induction phase is a sharp decrease in model size, and a moderate increase in data size, with the overall size constantly decreasing. Note that, although the number of rules rises, the total description length decreases. Again, this is precisely what we expected. The size of the model learned according to Saers *et al.* (2012) is close to 30 Mbits—far off the chart. This shows that our new top-down approach is indeed learning a more parsimonious grammar than the bottom-up approach.

Figures 3 and 4 shows the translation quality of the learned model. The thin flat lines show the quality of the bottom-up approach (Saers *et al.*, 2012), whereas the thick curves shows the quality of the new, top-down model presented in this paper without (dotted line), and without the bottom-up model (solid line). Although the MDL-based model is better than the old model, the combination of the two is still superior. It is particularly encouraging to see that the over-fitting that seems to take place after iteration 3 with the MDL-based approach is ameliorated with the bottom-up model.

8 Conclusions

We have introduced a purely unsupervised learning scheme for phrasal stochastic inversion transduction grammars that is the first to combine two opposing ways of searching for the phrasal translations: a bottom-up rule chunking approach driven by a maximum likelihood (ML) objective and a top-down rule segmenting approach driven by a minimum description length (MDL) objective. The combination approach takes advantage of the fact that the conservative top-down MDL-driven rule segmenting approach learns a very parsimonious, yet competitive, model when compared to a liberal bottom-up ML-driven approach. Results show that the combination of the two opposing approaches is significantly superior to either of them in isolation.

9 Acknowledgements

This material is based upon work supported in part by the Defense Advanced Research Projects Agency (DARPA) under BOLT contract no. HR0011-12-C-0016, and GALE contract nos. HR0011-06-C-0022 and HR0011-06-C-0023; by the European Union under the FP7 grant agreement no. 287658; and by the Hong Kong Research Grants Council (RGC) research grants GRF620811, GRF621008, and GRF612806. Any opinions, findings and conclusions or recommendations expressed in this material are those of the authors and do not necessarily reflect the views of DARPA, the EU, or RGC.

References

P. Blunsom and T. Cohn. Inducing synchronous grammars with slice sampling. In *HLT/NAACL2010*, pages 238–241, Los Angeles, California, June 2010.

P. Blunsom, T. Cohn, and M. Osborne. Bayesian synchronous grammar induction. In *Proceedings of NIPS 21*, Vancouver, Canada, December 2008.

P. Blunsom, T. Cohn, C. Dyer, and M. Osborne. A gibbs sampler for phrasal synchronous grammar induction. In *Proceedings of ACL/IJCNLP*, pages 782–790, Suntec, Singapore, August 2009.

P. F. Brown, S. A. Della Pietra, V. J. Della Pietra, and R. L. Mercer. The Mathematics of Machine Translation: Parameter estimation. *Computational Linguistics*, 19(2):263–311, 1993.

C. Cherry and D. Lin. Inversion transduction grammar for joint phrasal translation modeling. In *Proceedings of SSST*, pages 17–24, Rochester, New York, April 2007.

D. Chiang. Hierarchical phrase-based translation. *Computational Linguistics*, 33(2):201–228, 2007.

J. Cocke. *Programming languages and their compilers: Preliminary notes*. Courant Institute of Mathematical Sciences, New York University, 1969.

A. P. Dempster, N. M. Laird, and D. B. Rubin. Maximum likelihood from incomplete data via the em algorithm. *Journal of the Royal Statistical Society. Series B (Methodological)*, 39(1):1–38, 1977.

G. Doddington. Automatic evaluation of machine translation quality using n-gram co-occurrence statistics. In *Proceedings of the 2nd International Conference on Human Language Technology Research*, pages 138–145, San Diego, California, 2002.

C. S. Fordyce. Overview of the IWSLT 2007 evaluation campaign. In *Proceedings of IWSLT*, pages 1–12, 2007.

M. Galley, J. Graehl, K. Knight, D. Marcu, S. DeNeefe, W. Wang, and I. Thayer. Scalable inference and training of context-rich syntactic translation models. In *Proceedings of COLING/ACL-2006*, pages 961–968, Sydney, Australia, July 2006.

Peter Grünwald. A minimum description length approach to grammar inference in symbolic. *Lecture Notes in Artificial Intelligence*, (1040):203–216, 1996.

A. Haghighi, J. Blitzer, J. DeNero, and D. Klein. Better word alignments with supervised itg models. In *Proceedings of ACL/IJCNLP-2009*, pages 923–931, Suntec, Singapore, August 2009.

H. Johnson, J. Martin, G. Foster, and R. Kuhn. Improving translation quality by discarding most of the phrasetable. In *Proceedings of EMNLP-CoNLL-2007*, pages 967–975, Prague, Czech Republic, June 2007.

T. Kasami. An efficient recognition and syntax analysis algorithm for context-free languages. Technical Report AFCRL-65-00143, Air Force Cambridge Research Laboratory, 1965.

P. Koehn, F. J. Och, and D. Marcu. Statistical Phrase-Based Translation. In *Proceedings of HLT/NAACL-2003*, volume 1, pages 48–54, Edmonton, Canada, May/June 2003.

G. Neubig, T. Watanabe, E. Sumita, S. Mori, and T. Kawahara. An unsupervised model for joint phrase alignment and extraction. In *Proceedings of ACL/HLT-2011*, pages 632–641, Portland, Oregon, June 2011.

G. Neubig, T. Watanabe, S. Mori, and T. Kawahara. Machine translation without words through substring alignment. In *Proceedings of ACL-2012*, pages 165–174, Jeju Island, Korea, July 2012.

F. J. Och and H. Ney. A Systematic Comparison of Various Statistical Alignment Models. *Computational Linguistics*, 29(1):19–51, 2003.

F. J. Och. Minimum error rate training in statistical machine translation. In *Proceedings of ACL-2003*, pages 160–167, Sapporo, Japan, July 2003.

K. Papineni, S. Roukos, T. Ward, and W. Zhu. BLEU: a method for automatic evaluation of machine translation. In *Proceedings of ACL-2002*, pages 311–318, Philadelphia, Pennsylvania, July 2002.

J. Rissanen. A universal prior for integers and estimation by minimum description length. *The Annals of Statistics*, 11(2):416–431, June 1983.

M. Saers and D. Wu. Improving phrase-based translation via word alignments from Stochastic Inversion Transduction Grammars. In *Proceedings of SSST-3*, pages 28–36, Boulder, Colorado, June 2009.

M. Saers and D. Wu. Principled induction of phrasal bilexica. In *Proceedings of EAMT-2011*, pages 313–320, Leuven, Belgium, May 2011.

M. Saers, J. Nivre, and D. Wu. Learning stochastic bracketing inversion transduction grammars with a cubic time biparsing algorithm. In *Proceedings of IWPT'09*, pages 29–32, Paris, France, October 2009.

M. Saers, J. Nivre, and D. Wu. Word alignment with stochastic bracketing linear inversion transduction grammar. In *Proceedings of HLT/NAACL-2010*, pages 341–344, Los Angeles, California, June 2010.

M. Saers, K. Addanki, and D. Wu. From finite-state to inversion transductions: Toward unsupervised bilingual grammar induction. In *Proceedings of COLING 2012: Technical Papers*, pages 2325–2340, Mumbai, India, December 2012.

C. E. Shannon. A mathematical theory of communication. *The Bell System Technical Journal*, 27:379–423, 623–, July, October 1948.

Z. Si, M. Pei, B. Yao, and S. Zhu. Unsupervised learning of event and-or grammar and semantics from video. In *Proceedings of the 2011 IEEE International Conference on Computer Vision (ICCV)*, pages 41–48, November 2011.

R. J. Solomonoff. A new method for discovering the grammars of phrase structure languages. In *IFIP Congress*, pages 285–289, 1959.

A. Stolcke and S. Omohundro. Inducing probabilistic grammars by bayesian model merging. In R. C. Carrasco and J. Oncina, editors, *Grammatical Inference and Applications*, pages 106–118. Springer, 1994.

A. Stolcke. SRILM – an extensible language modeling toolkit. In *Proceedings of ICSLP-2002*, pages 901–904, Denver, Colorado, September 2002.

J. M. Vilar and E. Vidal. A recursive statistical translation model. In *ACL-2005 Workshop on Building and Using Parallel Texts*, pages 199–207, Ann Arbor, Jun 2005.

S. Vogel, H. Ney, and C. Tillmann. HMM-based Word Alignment in Statistical Translation. In *Proceedings of COLING-96*, volume 2, pages 836–841, 1996.

D. Wu. Stochastic Inversion Transduction Grammars and Bilingual Parsing of Parallel Corpora. *Computational Linguistics*, 23(3):377–403, 1997.

Z. Wu. LDC Chinese segmenter, 1999.

D. H. Younger. Recognition and parsing of context-free languages in time n^3. *Information and Control*, 10(2):189–208, 1967.

O. F. Zaidan. Z-MERT: A Fully Configurable Open Source Tool for Minimum Error Rate Training of Machine Translation Systems. *The Prague Bulletin of Mathematical Linguistics*, 91:79–88, 2009.

H. Zhang, C. Quirk, R. C. Moore, and D. Gildea. Bayesian learning of non-compositional phrases with synchronous parsing. In *Proceedings of ACL-08: HLT*, pages 97–105, Columbus, Ohio, June 2008.

A Formal Characterization of Parsing Word Alignments by Synchronous Grammars with Empirical Evidence to the ITG Hypothesis

Gideon Maillette de Buy Wenniger*
University of Amsterdam
gemdbw@gmail.com

Khalil Sima'an*
University of Amsterdam
k.simaan@uva.nl

Abstract

Deciding whether a synchronous grammar formalism generates a given word alignment (the *alignment coverage problem*) depends on finding an adequate instance grammar and then using it to parse the word alignment. *But what does it mean to parse a word alignment by a synchronous grammar?* This is formally undefined until we define an unambiguous mapping between grammatical derivations and word-level alignments. This paper proposes an initial, formal characterization of alignment coverage as intersecting two *partially ordered sets (graphs)* of translation equivalence units, one derived by a grammar instance and another defined by the word alignment. As a first sanity check, we report extensive coverage results for ITG on automatic and manual alignments. Even for the ITG formalism, our formal characterization makes explicit many algorithmic choices often left underspecified in earlier work.

1 Introduction

The training data used by current statistical machine translation (SMT) models consists of source and target sentence pairs aligned together at the word level (*word alignments*). For the hierarchical and syntactically-enriched SMT models, e.g., (Chiang, 2007; Zollmann and Venugopal, 2006), this training data is used for extracting *statistically weighted Synchronous Context-Free Grammars (SCFGs)*. Formally speaking, a synchronous grammar defines a set of (source-target) sentence pairs derived synchronously by the grammar. Contrary to common belief, however, a synchronous grammar (see e.g., (Chiang, 2005; Satta and Peserico, 2005)) does not accept (or parse) word alignments. This is because a synchronous derivation generates a tree pair with a bijective binary relation (links) between their *nonterminal* nodes. For deciding whether a given word alignment is generated/accepted by a given synchronous grammar, it is necessary to *interpret* the synchronous derivations down to the lexical level. However, it is formally defined yet how to unambiguously interpret the synchronous derivations of a synchronous grammar as word alignments. One major difficulty is that synchronous productions, in their most general form, may contain *unaligned* terminal sequences. Consider, for instance, the relatively non-complex synchronous production

$$\langle X \rightarrow \alpha\, X^{(1)}\, \beta\, X^{(2)}\, \gamma\, X^{(3)},\ X \rightarrow \sigma\, X^{(2)}\, \tau\, X^{(1)}\, \mu\, X^{(3)} \rangle$$

where superscript (i) stands for aligned instances of nonterminal X and all Greek symbols stand for arbitrary non-empty terminals sequences. Given a word aligned sentence pair it is necessary to bind the terminal sequence by alignments consistent with the given word alignment, and then parse the word alignment with the thus enriched grammar rules. This is not complex if we assume that each of the source terminal sequences is contiguously aligned with a target contiguous sequence, but difficult if we assume arbitrary alignments, including many-to-one and non-contiguously aligned chunks.

One important goal of this paper is to propose a formal characterization of what it means to synchronously parse a word alignment. Our formal characterization is borrowed from the "parsing as intersection" paradigm, e.g., (Bar-Hillel et al., 1964; Lang, 1988; van Noord, 1995; Nederhof and Satta,

* Institute for Logic, Language and Computation.

2004). Conceptually, our characterization makes use of three algorithms. Firstly, parse the *unaligned* sentence pair with the synchronous grammar to obtain a set of synchronous derivations, i.e., trees. Secondly, interpret a word alignment as generating a set of synchronous trees representing the recursive translation equivalence relations of interest[1] perceived in the word alignment. And finally, *intersect* the sets of nodes in the two sets of synchronous trees to check whether the grammar can generate (parts of) the word alignment. The formal detail of each of these three steps is provided in sections 3 to 5.

We think that alignment parsing is relevant for current research because it highlights the difference between alignments in training data and alignments accepted by a synchronous grammar (learned from data). This is useful for literature on learning from word aligned parallel corpora (e.g., (Zens and Ney, 2003; DeNero et al., 2006; Blunsom et al., 2009; Cohn and Blunsom, 2009; Riesa and Marcu, 2010; Mylonakis and Sima'an, 2011; Haghighi et al., 2009; McCarley et al., 2011)). A theoretical, formalized characterization of the alignment parsing problem is likely to improve the choices made in empirical work as well. We exemplify our claims by providing yet another empirical study of the stability of the ITG hypothesis. Our study highlights some of the technical choices left implicit in preceding work as explained in the next section.

2 First application to the ITG hypothesis

A grammar *formalism* is a whole set/family of synchronous grammars. For example, ITG (Wu, 1997) defines a family of *inversion-transduction grammars* differing among them in the exact set of synchronous productions, terminals and non-terminals. Given a synchronous grammar *formalism* and an input word alignment, a relevant theoretical question is *whether there exists an instance synchronous grammar* that generates the word alignment exactly. We will refer to this question as the *alignment coverage* problem. In this paper we propose an approach to the alignment coverage problem using the three-step solution proposed above for parsing word alignments by arbitrary synchronous grammars.

Most current use of synchronous grammars is limited to a subclass using a pair of nonterminals, e.g., (Chiang, 2007; Zollmann and Venugopal, 2006; Mylonakis and Sima'an, 2011), thereby remaining within the confines of the ITG formalism (Wu, 1997). On the one hand, this is because of computational complexity reasons. On the other, this choice relies on existing empirical evidence of what we will call the "ITG hypothesis", freely rephrased as follows: the ITG formalism is sufficient for representing a major percentage of reorderings in translation data in general.

Although checking whether a word alignment can be generated by ITG is far simpler than for arbitrary synchronous grammars, there is a striking variation in the approaches taken in the existing literature, e.g., (Zens and Ney, 2003; Wellington et al., 2006; Søgaard and Wu, 2009; Carpuat and Wu, 2007; Søgaard and Kuhn, 2009; Søgaard, 2010). Søgaard and Wu (Søgaard and Wu, 2009) observe justifiably that the literature studying the ITG alignment coverage makes conflicting choices in method and data, and reports significantly diverging alignment coverage scores. We hypothesize here that the major conflicting choices in method (what to count and how to parse) are likely due to the absence of a well-understood, formalized method for parsing word alignments even under ITG. In this paper we apply our formal approach to the ITG case, contributing new empirical evidence concerning the ITG hypothesis.

For our empirical study we exemplify our approach by detailing an algorithm dedicated to ITG in Normal-Form (NF-ITG). While our algorithm is in essence equivalent to existing algorithms for checking binarizability of permutations, e.g.,(Wu, 1997; Huang et al., 2009), the formal foundations preceding it concern nailing down the choices made in parsing arbitrary word alignments, as opposed to (bijective) permutations. The formalization is our way to resolve some of the major points of differences in existing literature.

We report new coverage results for ITG parsing of manual as well as automatic alignments, showing the contrast between the two kinds. While the latter seems built for phrase extraction, trading-off precision for recall, the former is heavily marked with id-

[1]The translation equivalence relations of interest may vary in kind as we will exemplify later. The known phrase pairs are merely one possible kind.

iomatic expressions. Our coverage results make explicit a relevant dilemma. To hierarchically parse the current automatic word alignments *exactly*, we will need more general synchronous reordering mechanisms than ITG, with increased risk of exponential parsing algorithms (Wu, 1997; Satta and Peserico, 2005). But if we abandon these word alignments, we will face the exponential problem of learning reordering arbitrary permutations, cf. (Tromble and Eisner, 2009). Our results also exhibit the importance of explicitly defining the units of translation equivalence when studying (ITG) coverage of word alignments. The more complex the choice of translation equivalence relations, the more difficult it is to parse the word alignments.

3 Translation equivalence in MT

In (Koehn et al., 2003), a translation equivalence unit (TEU) is a *phrase pair*: a pair of contiguous substrings of the source and target sentences such that the words on the one side align only with words on the other side (formal definitions next). The hierarchical phrase pairs (Chiang, 2005; Chiang, 2007) are extracted by replacing one or more sub-phrase pairs, that are contained within a phrase pair, by pairs of linked variables. This defines a subsumption relation between hierarchical phrase pairs (Zhang et al., 2008). Actual systems, e.g., (Koehn et al., 2003; Chiang, 2007) set an upperbound on length or the number of variables in the synchronous productions. For the purposes of our theoretical study, these practical limitations are irrelevant.

We give two definitions of translation equivalence for word alignments.[2] The first one makes no assumptions about the contiguity of TEUs, while the second does require them to be contiguous substrings on both sides (i.e., phrase pairs).

As usual, $\mathbf{s} = s_1...s_m$ and $\mathbf{t} = t_1...t_n$ are source and target sentences respectively. Let $\mathbf{s}_\sigma$ be the source word at position σ in $\mathbf{s}$ and $\mathbf{t}_\tau$ be the target word at position τ in $\mathbf{t}$. An alignment link $a \in \mathbf{a}$ in a word alignment $\mathbf{a}$ is a pair of positions $\langle\sigma, \tau\rangle$ such that $1 \leq \sigma \leq m$ and $1 \leq \tau \leq n$. For the sake of brevity, we will often talk about alignments without explicitly mentioning the associated source and target words, knowing that these can be readily obtained from the pair of positions and the sentence pair $\langle\mathbf{s}, \mathbf{t}\rangle$. Given a subset $\mathbf{a}' \subseteq \mathbf{a}$ we define $words_{\mathbf{s}}(\mathbf{a}') = \{\mathbf{s}_\sigma \mid \exists X : \langle\sigma, X\rangle \in \mathbf{a}'\}$ and $words_{\mathbf{t}}(\mathbf{a}') = \{\mathbf{t}_\tau \mid \exists X : \langle X, \tau\rangle \in \mathbf{a}'\}$.

Now we consider triples $(\mathbf{s}', \mathbf{t}', \mathbf{a}')$ such that $\mathbf{a}' \subseteq \mathbf{a}$, $\mathbf{s}' = words_{\mathbf{s}}(\mathbf{a}')$ and $\mathbf{t}' = words_{\mathbf{t}}(\mathbf{a}')$. We define the *translation equivalence units (TEUs)* in the set $\mathbf{TE}(\mathbf{s}, \mathbf{t}, \mathbf{a})$ as follows:

Definition 3.1 $(\mathbf{s}', \mathbf{t}', \mathbf{a}') \in \mathbf{TE}(\mathbf{s}, \mathbf{t}, \mathbf{a})$ *iff* $\langle\sigma, \tau\rangle \in \mathbf{a}'$ $\Rightarrow$ *(for all X, if* $\langle\sigma, X\rangle \in \mathbf{a}$ *then* $\langle\sigma, X\rangle \in \mathbf{a}'$*)* $\wedge$ *(for all X, if* $\langle X, \tau\rangle \in \mathbf{a}$ *then* $\langle X, \tau\rangle \in \mathbf{a}'$*)*

In other words, if some alignment involving source position σ or τ is included in $\mathbf{a}'$, then all alignments in $\mathbf{a}$ containing that position are in $\mathbf{a}'$ as well. This definition allows a variety of complex word alignments such as the so-called *Cross-serial Discontiguous Translation Units* and *Bonbons* (Søgaard and Wu, 2009).

We also define the subsumption relation (partial order) $<_{\mathbf{a}}$ as follows:

Definition 3.2 *A TEU* $u_2 = (\mathbf{s}_2, \mathbf{t}_2, \mathbf{a}_2)$ *subsumes* ($<_{\mathbf{a}}$) *a TEU* $u_1 = (\mathbf{s}_1, \mathbf{t}_1, \mathbf{a}_1)$ *iff* $\mathbf{a}_1 \subset \mathbf{a}_2$. *The subsumption order will be represented by* $u_1 <_{\mathbf{a}} u_2$.

Based on the subsumption relation we can partition $\mathbf{TE}(\mathbf{s}, \mathbf{t}, \mathbf{a})$ into two disjoint sets : atomic $\mathbf{TE}_{\mathbf{Atom}}(\mathbf{s}, \mathbf{t}, \mathbf{a})$ and composed $\mathbf{TE}_{\mathbf{Comp}}(\mathbf{s}, \mathbf{t}, \mathbf{a})$.

Definition 3.3 $u_1 \in \mathbf{TE}(\mathbf{s}, \mathbf{t}, \mathbf{a})$ *is* atomic *iff* $\nexists\, u_2 \in \mathbf{TE}(\mathbf{s}, \mathbf{t}, \mathbf{a})$ *such that* $(u_2 <_{\mathbf{a}} u_1)$.

Now the set $\mathbf{TE}_{\mathbf{Atom}}(\mathbf{s}, \mathbf{t}, \mathbf{a})$ is simply the set of all atomic translation equivalents, and the set of composed translation equivalents $\mathbf{TE}_{\mathbf{Comp}}(\mathbf{s}, \mathbf{t}, \mathbf{a}) = (\mathbf{TE}(\mathbf{s}, \mathbf{t}, \mathbf{a}) \setminus \mathbf{TE}_{\mathbf{Atom}}(\mathbf{s}, \mathbf{t}, \mathbf{a}))$.

Based on the general definition of translation equivalence, we can now give a more restricted definition that allows only contiguous translation equivalents (phrase pairs):

Definition 3.4 $(\mathbf{s}', \mathbf{t}', \mathbf{a}')$ *constitutes a* contiguous translation equivalent *iff:*

1. $(\mathbf{s}', \mathbf{t}', \mathbf{a}') \in \mathbf{TE}(\mathbf{s}, \mathbf{t}, \mathbf{a})$ *and*

[2] Unaligned words tend to complicate the formalization unnecessarily. As usual we also require that unaligned words must first be grouped with aligned words adjacent to them before translation equivalence is defined for an alignment. This standard strategy allows us to informally discuss unaligned words in the following without loss of generality.

2. *Both* $\mathbf{s}'$ *and* $\mathbf{t}'$ *are contiguous substrings of* $\mathbf{s}$ *and* $\mathbf{t}'$ *respectively.*

This set of translation equivalents is the unlimited set of phrase pairs known from phrase-based machine translation (Koehn et al., 2003). The relation $<_{\mathbf{a}}$ as well as the division into atomic and composed TEUs can straightforwardly be adapted to contiguous translation equivalents.

4 Grammatical translation equivalence

The derivations of a synchronous grammar can be interpreted as deriving a partially ordered set of TEUs as well. A finite derivation $S \rightarrow^{+} \langle \mathbf{s}, \mathbf{t}, \mathbf{a}_G \rangle$ of an instance grammar G is a finite sequence of term-rewritings, where at each step of the sequence a single nonterminal is rewritten using a synchronous production of G. The set of the finite derivations of G defines a language, a set of triples $\langle \mathbf{s}, \mathbf{t}, \mathbf{a}_G \rangle$ consisting of a source string of terminals $\mathbf{s}$, a target string of terminals $\mathbf{t}$ and an alignment between their grammatical constituents. Crucially, the alignment $\mathbf{a}_G$ is obtained by *recursively interpreting* the alignment relations embedded in the synchronous grammar productions in the derivation for all constituents and concerns constituent alignments (as opposed to word alignments).

Grammatical translation equivalents $\mathbf{TE}_G(\mathbf{s}, \mathbf{t})$ A synchronous derivation $S \rightarrow^{+} \langle \mathbf{s}, \mathbf{t}, \mathbf{a}_G \rangle$ can be viewed as a deductive proof that $\langle \mathbf{s}, \mathbf{t}, \mathbf{a}_G \rangle$ is a *grammatical* translation equivalence unit (grammatical TEU). Along the way, a derivation also proves other *constituent-level* (sub-sentential) units as TEUs.

We define a *sub-sentential* grammatical TEU of $\langle \mathbf{s}, \mathbf{t}, \mathbf{a}_G \rangle$ to consist of a triple $\langle \mathbf{s}_x, \mathbf{t}_x, \mathbf{a}_x \rangle$, where $\mathbf{s}_x$ and $\mathbf{t}_x$ are two *subsequences*[3] (of $\mathbf{s}$ and $\mathbf{t}$ respectively), derived synchronously from the same constituent X in some non-empty "tail" of a derivation $S \rightarrow^{+} \langle \mathbf{s}, \mathbf{t}, \mathbf{a}_G \rangle$; importantly, by the workings of G, the alignment $\mathbf{a}_x \subseteq \mathbf{a}_G$ fulfills the requirement that a word in $\mathbf{s}_x$ or in $\mathbf{t}_x$ is linked to another by $\mathbf{a}_G$ iff it is also linked that way by $\mathbf{a}_x$ (i.e., no alignments start out from terminals in $\mathbf{s}_x$ or $\mathbf{t}_x$ and link to terminals outside them). We will denote with $\mathbf{TE}_G(\mathbf{s}, \mathbf{t})$ the *set of all grammatical TEUs* for the sentence pair $\langle \mathbf{s}, \mathbf{t} \rangle$ derived by G.

Subsumption relation $<_{G(\mathbf{s},\mathbf{t})}$ Besides deriving TEUs, a derivation also shows *how* the different TEUs *compose* together into larger TEUs according to the grammar. We are interested in the *subsumption relation*: one grammatical TEU/constituent (u_1) subsumes another (u_2) (written $u_2 <_{G(\mathbf{s},\mathbf{t})} u_1$) iff the latter ($u_2$) is derived within a finite derivation of the former (u_1).[4]

The set of grammatical TEUs for a finite set of derivations for a given sentence pair is the union of the sets defined for the individual derivations. Similarly, the relation between TEU's for a set of derivations is defined as the union of the individual relations.

5 Alignment coverage by intersection

Let a word aligned sentence pair $\langle \mathbf{s}, \mathbf{t}, \mathbf{a} \rangle$ be given, and let us assume that we have a definition of an ordered set $\mathbf{TE}(\mathbf{s}, \mathbf{t}, \mathbf{a})$ with partial order $<_{\mathbf{a}}$. We will say that a *grammar formalism covers* $\mathbf{a}$ iff there exists an instance grammar G that fulfills two intersection equations simultaneously:[5]

$$\textbf{(1)}\quad \mathbf{TE}(\mathbf{s}, \mathbf{t}, \mathbf{a}) \cap \mathbf{TE}_G(\mathbf{s}, \mathbf{t}) = \mathbf{TE}(\mathbf{s}, \mathbf{t}, \mathbf{a})$$

$$\textbf{(2)}\quad <_{\mathbf{a}} \cap <_{G(\mathbf{s},\mathbf{t})} = <_{\mathbf{a}}$$

In the second equation, the intersection of partial orders is based on the standard view that these are in essence also sets of ordered pairs. In practice, it is sufficient to implement an algorithm that shows

[3]A subsequence of a string is a subset of the word-position pairs that preserves the order but do not necessarily constitute contiguous substrings.

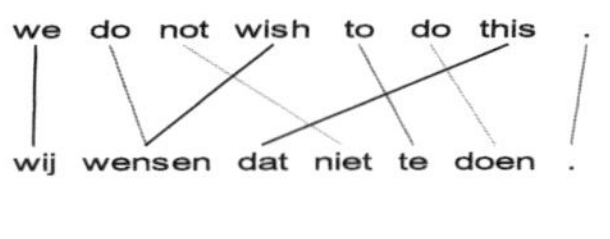

Figure 2: Alignment with both contiguous and discontiguous TEUs (example from Europarl En-Ne).

[4]Note that we define this relation exhaustively thereby defining the set of paths in synchronous trees derived by the grammar for $\langle \mathbf{s}, \mathbf{t} \rangle$. Hence, the subsumption relation can be seen to define a forest of synchronous trees.

[5]In this work we have restricted this definition to full coverage (i.e., subset) version but it is imaginable that other measures can be based on the cardinality (size) of the intersection in terms of covered TEUs, in following of measures found in (Søgaard and Kuhn, 2009; Søgaard and Wu, 2009). We leave this to future work.

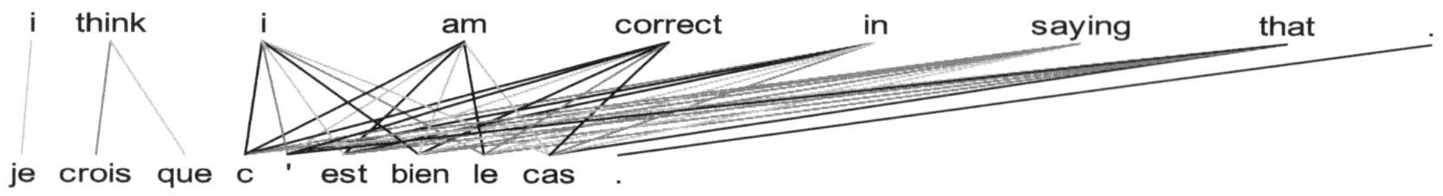

Figure 1: Alignment with only contiguous TEUs (example from LREC En-Fr).

that G *derives every TEU* in $\mathbf{TE}(\mathbf{s},\mathbf{t},\mathbf{a})$, and that the subsumption relation $<_\mathbf{a}$ between TEUs in $\mathbf{a}$ must be realized by the derivations of G that derive $\mathbf{TE}(\mathbf{s},\mathbf{t},\mathbf{a})$. In effect, this way every TEU that subsumes other TEUs must be derived recursively, while the minimal, atomic units (not subsuming any others) must be derived using the lexical productions (endowed with internal word alignments) of NF-ITG. Again, the rationale behind this choice is that the atomic units constitute fixed translation expressions (idiomatic TEUs) which cannot be composed from other TEUs, and hence belong in the lexicon. We will exhibit coverage algorithms for doing so for NF-ITG for the two kinds of semantic interpretations of word alignments.

A note on dedicated instances of NF-ITG Given a translation equivalence definition over word alignments $\mathbf{TE}(\mathbf{s},\mathbf{t},\mathbf{a})$, the lexical productions for a *dedicated* instance of NF-ITG are defined[6] by the set $\{X \rightarrow u \mid u \in \mathbf{TE_{Atom}}(\mathbf{s},\mathbf{t},\mathbf{a})\}$. This means that the lexical productions have atomic TEUs at the right-hand side including alignments between the words of the source and target terminals. In the sequel, we will only talk about dedicated instances of NF-ITG and hence we will not explicitly repeat this every time.

Given two grammatical TEUs u_1 and u_2, an NF-ITG instance allows their concatenation either in monotone [] or inverted <> order iff they are adjacent on the source and target sides. This fact implies that for every composed translation equivalent $u \in \mathbf{TE}(\mathbf{s},\mathbf{t},\mathbf{a})$ we can check whether it is derivable by a dedicated NF-ITG instance by checking whether it recursively decomposes into adjacent pairs of TEUs down to the atomic TEUs level. Note that by doing so, we are also implicitly checking whether the subsumption order between the TEUs in $\mathbf{TE}(\mathbf{s},\mathbf{t},\mathbf{a})$ is realized by the grammatical derivation (i.e, $<_{G(\mathbf{s},\mathbf{t})} \subseteq <_\mathbf{a}$). Formally, an aligned sentence pair $\langle \mathbf{s},\mathbf{t},\mathbf{a}\rangle$ is split into a pair of TEUs $\langle \mathbf{s}_1,\mathbf{t}_1,\mathbf{a}_1\rangle$ and $\langle \mathbf{s}_2,\mathbf{t}_2,\mathbf{a}_2\rangle$ that can be composed back using the [] and <> productions. If such a split exists, the splitting is conducted recursively for each of $\langle \mathbf{s}_1,\mathbf{t}_1,\mathbf{a}_1\rangle$ and $\langle \mathbf{s}_2,\mathbf{t}_2,\mathbf{a}_2\rangle$ until both are atomic TEUs in $\mathbf{TE}(\mathbf{s},\mathbf{t},\mathbf{a})$. This recursive splitting is the check of *binarizability* and an algorithm is described in (Huang et al., 2009).

6 A simple algorithm for ITG

We exemplify the grammatical coverage for (normal form) ITG by employing a standard tabular algorithm based on CYK (Younger, 1967). The algorithm works in two phases creating a chart containing TEUs with associated inferences. In the initialization phase (Algorithm 1), for all source spans that correspond to translation equivalents and which have no smaller translation equivalents they contain, *atomic translation equivalents* are added as atomic inferences to the chart. In the second phase, based on the atomic inferences, the simple rules of NF-ITG are applied to add inferences for increasingly larger chart entries. An inference is added (Algorithms 2 and 3) iff a chart entry can be split into two sub-entries for which inferences already exist, and furthermore the union of the sets of target positions for those two entries form a consecutive range.[7] The *addMonotoneInference* and *addInvertedInference* in Algorithm 3 mark the composit inferences by monotone and inverted productions respectively.

[6]Unaligned words add one wrinkle in this scheme: informally, we consider a TEU u formed by attaching unaligned words to an atomic TEU also as atomic iff u is absolutely needed to cover the aligned sentence pair.

[7]We are not treating unaligned words formally here. For unaligned source and target words, we have to generate the different inferences corresponding to different groupings with their neighboring aligned words. Using pre-processing we set aside the unaligned words, then parse the remaining word alignment fully. After parsing, by post-processing, we introduce in the parse table atomic TEUs that include the unaligned words.

```
InitializeChart
Input  : ⟨s, t, a⟩
Output: Initialized chart for atomic units

for spanLength ← 2 to n do
    for i ← 0 to n − spanLength + 1 do
        j ← i + spanLength − 1
        u ← {⟨X, Y⟩ : X ∈ {i...j}}
        if (u ∈ TE_Atom(s, t, a)) then
            addAtomicInference(chart[i][j], u)
        end
    end
end
```

Algorithm 1: Algorithm that initializes the Chart with atomic sub-sentential TEUs. In order to be atomic, a TEU may not contain smaller TEUs that consist of a proper subset of the alignments (and associated words) of the TEU.

```
ComputeTEUsNFITG
Input  : ⟨s, t, a⟩
Output: TRUE/FALSE for coverage

InitializeChart(chart)
for spanLength ← 2 to n do
    for i ← 0 to n − spanLength + 1 do
        j ← i + spanLength − 1
        if chart[i][j] ∈ TE(s, t, a) then
            continue
        end
        for splitPoint ← i + 1 to j do
            a′ ← (chart[i][k − 1] ∪ chart[k][j])
            if (chart[i][k − 1] ∈ TE(s, t, a)) ∧
            (chart[k][j] ∈ TE(s, t, a)) ∧
            (a′ ∈ TE(s, t, a)) then
                addTEU(chart, i, j, k, a′)
            end
        end
    end
    if (chart[0][n − 1] ≠ ∅) then
        return TRUE
    else
        return FALSE
    end
end
```

Algorithm 2: Algorithm that incrementally builds composite TEUs using only the rules allowed by NF-ITG

```
addTEU
Input  :
 chart - the chart
 i,j,k - the lower, upper and split point indices
 a′ - the TEU to be added
Output: chart with TEU a′ added in the
        intended entry

if Max_{Y_t}({Y_t : ⟨X_s, Y_t⟩ ∈ chart[i][k − 1]})
< Max_{Y_t}({Y_t : ⟨X_s, Y_t⟩ ∈ chart[k][j]}) then
    addMonotoneInference(chart[i][j], a′)
else
    addInvertedInference(chart[i][j], a′)
end
```

Algorithm 3: Algorithm that adds a TEU and associated Inference to the chart

7 Experiments

Data Sets We use manually and automatically aligned corpora. Manually aligned corpora come from two datasets. The first (Graça et al., 2008) consists of six language pairs: Portuguese–English, Portuguese–French, Portuguese–Spanish, English–Spanish, English–French and French–Spanish. These datasets contain 100 sentence pairs each and distinguish *Sure* and *Possible* alignments. Following (Søgaard and Kuhn, 2009), we treat these two equally. The second manually aligned dataset (Padó and Lapata, 2006) contains 987 sentence pairs from the English-German part of Europarl annotated using the Blinker guidelines (Melamed, 1998). The automatically aligned data comes from Europarl (Koehn, 2005) in three language pairs (English–Dutch, English–French and English–German). The corpora are automatically aligned using GIZA++ (Och and Ney, 2003) in combination with the grow-diag-final-and heuristic. With sentence length cutoff 40 on both sides these contain respectively 945k, 949k and 995k sentence pairs.

Grammatical Coverage (GC) is defined as the percentage word alignments (sentence pairs) in a parallel corpus that can be covered by an instance of the grammar (NF-ITG) (cf. Section 5). Clearly, GC depends on the chosen semantic interpretation of word alignments: contiguous TE's (phrase pairs) or discontiguous TE's.

Alignments Set	GC contiguous TEs	GC discontiguous TEs
Hand aligned corpora		
English–French	76.0	75.0
English–Portuguese	78.0	78.0
English–Spanish	83.0	83.0
Portuguese–French	78.0	74.0
Portuguese–Spanish	91.0	91.0
Spanish–French	79.0	74.0
LREC Corpora Average	80.83±5.49	79.17±6.74
English–German	45.427	45.325
Automatically aligned Corpora		
English–Dutch	45.533	43.57
English–French	52.84	49.95
English–German	45.59	43.72
Automatically aligned corpora average	47.99±4.20	45.75±3.64

Table 1: The grammatical coverage (GC) of NF-ITG for different corpora dependent on the interpretation of word alignments: contiguous Translation Equivalence or discontiguous Translation Equivalence

Results Table 1 shows the Grammatical Coverage (GC) of NF-ITG for the different corpora dependent on the two alternative definitions of *translation equivalence*. The first thing to notice is that there is just a small difference between the Grammatical Coverage scores for these two definitions. The difference is in the order of a few percentage points, the largest difference is seen for Portuguese–French (79% v.s 74% Grammatical Coverage), for some language pairs there is no difference. For the automatically aligned corpora the absolute difference is on average about 2%. We attribute this to the fact that there are only very few discontiguous TEUs that can be covered by NF-ITG in this data.

The second thing to notice is that the scores are much higher for the corpora from the LREC dataset than they are for the manually aligned English–German corpus. The approximately double source and target length of the manually aligned English–German corpus, in combination with somewhat less dense alignments makes this corpus much harder than the LREC corpora. Intuitively, one would expect that more alignment links make alignments more complicated. This turns out to not always be the case. Further inspection of the LREC alignments also shows that these alignments often consist of parts that are *completely linked*. Such completely linked parts are by definition treated as atomic TEUs, which could make the alignments look simpler. This contrasts with the situation in the manually aligned English–German corpus where on average less alignment links exist per word. Examples 1 and 2 show that dense alignments can be simpler than less dense ones. This is because sometimes the density implies idiomatic TEUs which leads to rather flat lexical productions. We think that idiomatic TEUs reasonably belong in the lexicon.

When we look at the results for the automatically aligned corpora at the lowest rows in the table, we see that these are comparable to the results for the manually aligned English–German corpus (and much lower than the results for the LREC corpora). This could be explained by the fact that the manually aligned English–German is not only Europarl data, but possibly also because the manual alignments themselves were obtained by initialization with the GIZA++ alignments. In any case, the manually and automatically acquired alignments for this data are not too different from the perspective of NF-ITG. Further differences might exist if we would employ another class of grammars, e.g., full SCFGs.

One the one hand, we find that manual alignments are well but not fully covered by NF-ITG. On the other, the automatic alignments are not covered well but NF-ITG. This suggests that these automatic alignments are difficult to cover by NF-ITG, and the reason could be that these alignments are built heuristically by trading precision for recall cf.

(Och and Ney, 2003). Sogaard (Søgaard, 2010) reports that full ITG provides a few percentage points gains over NF-ITG.

Overall, we find that our results for the LREC data are far higher Sogaard's (Søgaard, 2010) results but lower than the upperbounds of (Søgaard and Wu, 2009). A similar observation holds for the English–German manually aligned EuroParl data, albeit the maximum length (15) used in (Søgaard and Wu, 2009; Søgaard, 2010) is different from ours (40). We attribute the difference between our results and Sogaard's approach to our choice to adopt lexical productions of NF-ITG that contain own internal alignments (the detailed version) and determined by the atomic TEUs of the word alignment. Our results differ substantially from (Søgaard and Wu, 2009) who report upperbounds (indeed our results still fall within these upperbounds for the LREC data).

8 Related Work

The array of work described in (Zens and Ney, 2003; Wellington et al., 2006; Søgaard and Wu, 2009; Søgaard and Kuhn, 2009; Søgaard, 2010) concentrates on methods for calculating *upperbounds* on the alignment coverage for all ITGs, including NF-ITG. Interestingly, these upperbounds are determined by *filtering/excluding complex alignment phenomena* known formally to be beyond (NF-)ITG. None of these earlier efforts discussed explicitly the dilemmas of instantiating a grammar formalism or how to formally parse word alignments.

The work in (Zens and Ney, 2003; Søgaard and Wu, 2009), defining and counting TEUs, provides a far tighter upperbound than (Wellington et al., 2006), who use the disjunctive interpretation of word alignments, interpreting multiple alignment links of the same word as alternatives. We adopt the conjunctive interpretation of word alignments like a majority of work in MT, e.g., (Ayan and Dorr, 2006; Fox, 2002; Søgaard and Wu, 2009; Søgaard, 2010).

In deviation from earlier work, the work in (Søgaard and Kuhn, 2009; Søgaard and Wu, 2009; Søgaard, 2010) discusses TEUs defined over word alignments explicitly, and defines evaluation metrics based on TEUs. In particular, Sogaard (Søgaard, 2010) writes that he employs "a more aggressive search" for TEUs than earlier work, thereby leading to far tighter upperbounds on hand aligned data. Our results seem to back this claim but, unfortunately, we could not pin down the formal details of his procedure.

More remotely related, the work described in (Huang et al., 2009) presents a binarization algorithm for productions of an SCFG instance (as opposed to formalism). Although somewhat related, this is different from checking whether there exists an NF-ITG instance (which has to be determined) that covers a word alignment.

In contrast with earlier work, we present the alignment coverage problem as an intersection of two partially ordered sets (graphs). The partial order over TEUs as well as the formal definition of parsing as intersection in this work are novel elements, making explicit the view of word alignments as automata generating partially order sets.

9 Conclusions

In this paper we provide a formal characterization for the problem of determining the coverage of a word alignment by a given grammar formalism as the intersection of two partially ordered sets. These partially ordered set of TEUs can be formalized in terms of hyper-graphs implementing forests (packed synchronous trees), and the coverage as the intersection between sets of synchronous trees generalizing the trees of (Zhang et al., 2008).

Practical explorations of our findings for the benefit of models of learning reordering are underway. In future work we would like to investigate the extension of this work to other limited subsets of SCFGs. We will also investigate the possibility of devising ITGs with explicit links between terminal symbols in the productions, exploring different kinds of linking.

Acknowledgements We thank reviewers for their helpful comments, and thank Mark-Jan Nederhof for illuminating discussions on parsing as intersection. This work is supported by The Netherlands Organization for Scientific Research (NWO) under grant nr. 612.066.929.

References

Nacip Ayan and Bonnie Dorr. 2006. Going beyond AER: an extensive analysis of word alignments and their impact on MT. In *Proc. of the 21st International Conference on Computational Linguistics and the 44th Annual Meeting of the ACL*, pages 9–16, Morristown, NJ, USA.

Yehoshua Bar-Hillel, Micha Perles, and Eli Shamir. 1964. On formal properties of simple phrase structure grammars. In Y. Bar-Hillel, editor, *Language and Information: Selected Essays on their Theory and Application*, chapter 9, pages 116–150. Addison-Wesley, Reading, Massachusetts.

Phil Blunsom, Trevor Cohn, Chris Dyer, and Miles Osborne. 2009. A gibbs sampler for phrasal synchronous grammar induction. In *ACL/AFNLP*, pages 782–790.

Marine Carpuat and Dekai Wu. 2007. Improving statistical machine translation using word sense disambiguation. In *Proc. of the Joint Conference on Empirical Methods in Natural Language Processing and Computational Natural Language Learning (EMNLP-CoNLL 2007)*, page 61–72.

David Chiang. 2005. A hierarchical phrase-based model for statistical machine translation. In *Proceedings of the 43rd Annual Meeting of the ACL*, pages 263–270, June.

David Chiang. 2007. Hierarchical phrase-based translation. *Computational Linguistics*, 33(2):201–228.

Trevor Cohn and Phil Blunsom. 2009. A bayesian model of syntax-directed tree to string grammar induction. In *EMNLP*, pages 352–361.

John DeNero, Daniel Gillick, James Zhang, and Dan Klein. 2006. Why generative phrase models underperform surface heuristics. In *Proceedings of the workshop on SMT*, pages 31–38.

Heidi J. Fox. 2002. Phrasal cohesion and statistical machine translation. In *Proceedings of the ACL-02 conference on Empirical methods in natural language processing - Volume 10*, Proceedings of EMNLP, pages 304–311, Stroudsburg, PA, USA. Association for Computational Linguistics.

Joao Graça, Joana Pardal, Luísa Coheur, and Diamantino Caseiro. 2008. Building a golden collection of parallel multi-language word alignment. In *LREC'08*, Marrakech, Morocco. European Language Resources Association (ELRA).

Aria Haghighi, John Blitzer, John DeNero, and Dan Klein. 2009. Better word alignments with supervised itg models. In *Proceedings of the Joint Conference of the 47th Annual Meeting of the ACL and the 4th International Joint Conference on Natural Language Processing of the AFNLP*, pages 923–931, Suntec, Singapore, August. Association for Computational Linguistics.

Liang Huang, Hao Zhang, Daniel Gildea, and Kevin Knight. 2009. Binarization of synchronous context-free grammars. *Computational Linguistics*, 35(4):559–595.

Philipp Koehn, Franz Josef Och, and Daniel Marcu. 2003. Statistical phrase-based translation. In *Proc. of the Human Language Technology Conference, HLT-NAACL*, May.

Philipp Koehn. 2005. Europarl: A parallel corpus for statistical machine translation. In *Proc. of MT Summit*.

Bernard Lang. 1988. Parsing incomplete sentences. In *Proceedings of COLING*, pages 365–371.

J. Scott McCarley, Abraham Ittycheriah, Salim Roukos, Bing Xiang, and Jian-Ming Xu. 2011. A correction model for word alignments. In *Proceedings of EMNLP*, pages 889–898.

Dan Melamed. 1998. Annotation style guide for the blinker project, version 1.0. Technical Report IRCS TR #98-06, University of Pennsylvania.

Markos Mylonakis and Khalil Sima'an. 2011. Learning hierarchical translation structure with linguistic annotations. In *Proceedings of the HLT/NAACL-2011*.

Mark-Jan Nederhof and Giorgio Satta. 2004. The language intersection problem for non-recursive context-free grammars. *Inf. Comput.*, 192(2):172–184.

Franz Josef Och and Hermann Ney. 2003. A systematic comparison of various statistical alignment models. *Computational Linguistics*, 29(1):19–51.

Sebastian Padó and Mirella Lapata. 2006. Optimal constituent alignment with edge covers for semantic projection. In *ACL-COLING'06*, ACL-44, pages 1161–1168, Stroudsburg, PA, USA. Association for Computational Linguistics.

Jason Riesa and Daniel Marcu. 2010. Hierarchical search for word alignment. In *Proceedings of ACL*, pages 157–166.

Giorgio Satta and Enoch Peserico. 2005. Some computational complexity results for synchronous context-free grammars. In *Proceedings of Human Language Technology Conference and Conference on Empirical Methods i n Natural Language Processing*, pages 803–810, Vancouver, British Columbia, Canada, October. Association for Computational Linguistics.

Anders Søgaard and Jonas Kuhn. 2009. Empirical lower bounds on alignment error rates in syntax-based machine translation. In *SSST '09*, pages 19–27, Stroudsburg, PA, USA. Association for Computational Linguistics.

Anders Søgaard and Dekai Wu. 2009. Empirical lower bounds on translation unit error rate for the full class of inversion transduction grammars. In *Proceedings of the 11th International Workshop on Parsing Technologies (IWPT-2009), 7-9 October 2009, Paris, France,* pages 33–36. The Association for Computational Linguistics.

Anders Søgaard. 2010. Can inversion transduction grammars generate hand alignments? In *Proccedings of the 14th Annual Conference of the European Association for Machine Translation (EAMT)*.

Roy Tromble and Jason Eisner. 2009. Learning linear ordering problems for better translation. In *Proceedings of EMNLP'09*, pages 1007–1016, Singapore.

Gertjan van Noord. 1995. The intersection of finite state automata and definite clause grammars. In *Proceedings of ACL*, pages 159–165.

Benjamin Wellington, Sonjia Waxmonsky, and I. Dan Melamed. 2006. Empirical lower bounds on the complexity of translational equivalence. In *Proceedings of the Annual Meeting of the Association for Computational Linguistics (ACL)*.

Dekai Wu. 1997. Stochastic inversion transduction grammars and bilingual parsing of parallel corpora. *Computational Linguistics*, 3(23):377–403.

D.H. Younger. 1967. Recognition and parsing of context-free languages in time n^3. *Information and Control*, 10(2):189–208.

Richard Zens and Hermann Ney. 2003. A comparative study on reordering constraints in statistical machine translation. In *Proceedings of the Annual Meeting of the ACL*, pages 144–151.

Hao Zhang, Daniel Gildea, and David Chiang. 2008. Extracting synchronous grammar rules from word-level alignments in linear time. In *Proceedings of COLING*, pages 1081–1088.

Andreas Zollmann and Ashish Venugopal. 2006. Syntax augmented machine translation via chart parsing. In *Proceedings of the North-American Chapter of the ACL (NAACL'06)*, pages 138–141.

Synchronous Linear Context-Free Rewriting Systems for Machine Translation

Miriam Kaeshammer
University of Düsseldorf
Universitätsstraße 1
40225 Düsseldorf, Germany

Abstract

We propose synchronous linear context-free rewriting systems as an extension to synchronous context-free grammars in which synchronized non-terminals span $k \geq 1$ continuous blocks on each side of the bitext. Such discontinuous constituents are required for inducing certain alignment configurations that occur relatively frequently in manually annotated parallel corpora and that cannot be generated with less expressive grammar formalisms. As part of our investigations concerning the minimal k that is required for inducing manual alignments, we present a hierarchical aligner in form of a deduction system. We find that by restricting k to 2 on both sides, 100% of the data can be covered.

1 Introduction

The most prominent paradigms in statistical machine translation are phrase-based translation models (Koehn et al., 2003) and tree-based approaches using some form of a synchronous context-free grammar (SCFG) (Chiang, 2007; Zollmann and Venugopal, 2006; Hoang and Koehn, 2010), in particular inversion transduction grammar (ITG) (Wu, 1997). The rules of the translation models are usually learned from word aligned parallel corpora. Synchronous grammars also induce alignments between words in the bitext when simultaneously recognizing words via the application of a synchronous rule (Wu, 1997). Due to their central role, it is important that a synchronous grammar formalism is powerful enough to generate all alignment configurations that occur in hand-aligned parallel corpora that are taken to be a gold standard of translational equivalence (Wellington et al., 2006).

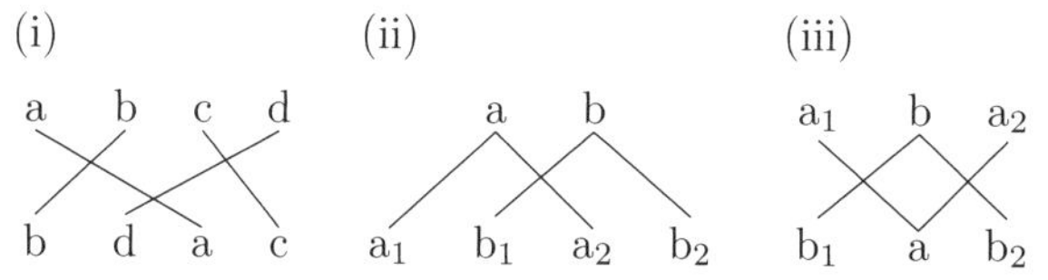

Figure 1: (i) inside-out alignment (Wu, 1997); (ii) cross-serial discontinuous translation unit (Søgaard and Kuhn, 2009); (iii) bonbon alignment (Simard et al., 2005)

The empirical adequacy of phrase-based and SCFG-based translation models has been put into question (Wellington et al., 2006; Søgaard and Kuhn, 2009; Søgaard and Wu, 2009; Søgaard, 2010) because they are unable to induce certain alignment configurations. In the alignments in Figure 1, the translation units *a*, *b*, *c*, and *d* cannot be independently generated by a binary SCFG. Due to a reordering component, phrase-based systems can handle (i), but neither (ii) nor (iii). Those phenomena however occur relatively frequently in hand-aligned parallel corpora. Wellington et al. (2006) found that complex structures such as inside-out alignments occur in 5% of English-Chinese sentence pairs and in the study of Søgaard and Kuhn (2009) between 1.6% (for Danish-English data) and 12.1% (for Danish-Spanish data) of all translation units are discontinuous, i.e. not derivable by ITGs in normal form.

As Wellington et al. (2006) already noted for inside-out alignments, *discontinuous constituents* are required for binary synchronous derivations of the alignment configurations under consideration. This is illustrated in Figure 2: the yields of $A_{\boxed{2}}$

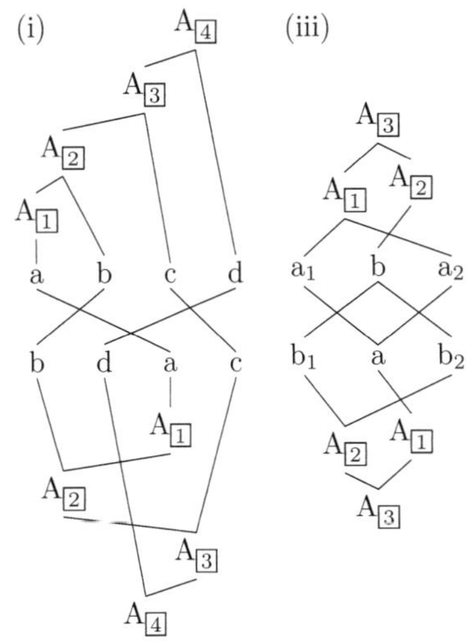

Figure 2: Synchronous derivations: co-indexed non-terminals are generated synchronously. Note that many other derivations that induce the same alignment structures are possible, but all of them involve at least one discontinuous constituent.

and $A_{\boxed{3}}$ in (i) are discontinuous on the target side, in (iii) the yield of $A_{\boxed{1}}$ is discontinuous on the source side and the yield of $A_{\boxed{2}}$ is discontinuous on the target side. We therefore propose to augment tree-based approaches such that they can account for discontinuous constituents in the source and/or target derivation. This implies going beyond the power of context-free grammars.

In the monolingual parsing community, linear context-free rewriting systems (LCFRS) have been established as an appropriate formalism for the modeling of discontinuous structure (Maier and Lichte, 2011; Kuhlmann and Satta, 2009). LCFRS is an extension of CFG, in which non-terminals can span $k \geq 1$ continuous blocks of a string. k is termed the *fan-out* of the non-terminal. If $k = 1$ for all non-terminals, the grammar is a CFG. Recent work shows that probabilistic data-driven parsing with LCFRS is indeed feasible and gives acceptable results (Maier, 2010; Evang and Kallmeyer, 2011; van Cranenburgh, 2012; Maier et al., 2012; Kallmeyer and Maier, 2013). It seems timely to transfer these findings to statistical machine translation.

In this work, we introduce the notion of synchronous LCFRS for translation and show how the alignments in Figure 1 are induced. Since the parsing complexity of LCFRS, and thus of synchronous LCFRS as well, depends directly on k, the number of blocks that a non-terminal in the grammar may span, an investigation concerning the empirically required k is carried out on manually aligned data. For this purpose, we present a parallel parser for an all-accepting synchronous LCFRS that is used to validate hierarchical alignments for a given k. This extends the work of Wellington et al. (2006) and Søgaard (2010) from a methodological point of view, as will be explained in Section 5. In particular, we will revise the results that Søgaard (2010) presented concerning the coverage of ITG. Our experiments furthermore include data sets that have not been used in previous similar studies.

2 Synchronous LCFRS for Translation

2.1 LCFRS

An LCFRS[1] (Vijay-Shanker et al., 1987; Weir, 1988) is a tuple $G = (N, T, V, P, S)$ where N is a finite set of non-terminals with a function dim: $N \to \mathbb{N}$ determining the *fan-out* of each $A \in N$; T and V are disjoint finite sets of terminals and variables; $S \in N$ is the start symbol with $dim(S) = 1$; and P is a finite set of rewriting rules

$$A(\alpha_1, \ldots, \alpha_{dim(A)}) \to A_1(X_1^{(1)}, \ldots, X_{dim(A_1)}^{(1)}) \cdots A_m(X_1^{(m)}, \ldots, X_{dim(A_m)}^{(m)})$$

where $A, A_1, \ldots, A_m \in N$, $X_j^{(i)} \in V$ for $1 \leq i \leq m$, $1 \leq j \leq dim(A_i)$ and $\alpha_i \in (T \cup V)^*$ for $1 \leq i \leq dim(A)$, for a *rank* $m \geq 0$. For all $r \in P$, every variable X in r occurs exactly once in the left-hand side (LHS) and exactly once in the right-hand side (RHS) of r. r describes how the yield of the LHS non-terminal is computed from the yields of the RHS non-terminals. The yield of S is the language of the grammar. Figure 3 shows a sample LCFRS with more explanations.

The *rank* of G is the maximal rank of any of its rules, and its *fan-out* is the maximal fan-out of any of its non-terminals. G is called a (u, v)-LCFRS if it has rank u and fan-out v.

2.2 Synchronous LCFRS

We define synchronous LCFRS (SLCFRS) in parallel to synchronous CFG, see for example Satta

[1]We use the syntax of simple range concatenation grammars (Boullier, 1998), a formalism that is equivalent to LCFRS.

$A(ab, cd) \rightarrow \varepsilon$	$\langle ab, cd \rangle$ in yield of A
$A(aXb, cYd) \rightarrow A(X, Y)$	if $\langle X, Y \rangle$ in yield of A, then also $\langle aXb, cYd \rangle$ in yield of A
$S(XY) \rightarrow A(X, Y)$	if $\langle X, Y \rangle$ in yield of A, then $\langle XY \rangle$ in yield of S

Figure 3: Sample LCFRS for $L = \{a^n b^n c^n d^n \mid n > 0\}$

and Peserico (2005). An SLCFRS is a tuple $G = (N_s, N_t, T_s, T_t, V_s, V_t, P, S_s, S_t)$ where N_s, T_s, V_s, S_s, resp. N_t, T_t, V_t, S_t are defined as for LCFRS. They denote the alphabets for the *source* and *target side* respectively. P is a finite set of synchronous rewriting rules $\langle r_s, r_t, \sim \rangle$ where r_s and r_t are LCFRS rewriting rules based on N_s, T_s, V_s and N_t, T_t, V_t respectively, and $\sim$ is a bijective mapping of the non-terminals in the RHS of r_s to the non-terminals in the RHS of r_t. This link relation is represented by co-indexation in the synchronous rules. During a derivation, the yields of two co-indexed non-terminals have to be explained from one synchronous rule. $\langle S_s, S_t \rangle$ is the start pair.

We call the tuple $(N_s, T_s, V_s, P_s, S_s)$ the *source side grammar* G_s and $(N_t, T_t, V_t, P_t, S_t)$ the *target side grammar* G_t where P_s is the set of all r_s in P and P_t is the set of all r_t in P. The *rank* u of G is the maximal rank of G_s and G_t, and the *fan-out* v of G is the sum of the fan-outs of G_s and G_t. We will sometimes write $v_{v_{G_s}|v_{G_t}}$ to make clear how the fan-out of G is distributed over the source and the target side. As in the monolingual case, a corresponding grammar G is called a (u, v)-SLCFRS.

As an example consider the rules in Figure 4. They translate cross-serial dependencies into nested ones. The rank of the corresponding grammar is 2 and its fan-out $4_{2|2}$.

Note that instead of defining an SLCFRS, one could also set the fan-out of each non-terminal in an LCFRS to ≥ 2, set $dim(S) = 2$, and formulate synchronization between the arguments of the non-terminals. The main disadvantage is that this requires $N_s = N_t$. Furthermore, this seems less perspicuous than SLCFRS when moving from SCFG to mild context-sensitivity. Generalized Multitext Grammar (Melamed et al., 2004) is another weakly equivalent grammar formalism.

In correspondence to ITG and normal-form ITG (NF-ITG) (Søgaard and Wu, 2009), we say an

$$
\begin{array}{ll}
\langle A(a, c) \rightarrow \varepsilon & , C(a, c) \rightarrow \varepsilon \rangle \\
\langle B(b, d) \rightarrow \varepsilon & , D(bd) \rightarrow \varepsilon \rangle \\
\langle A(aX, cZ) \rightarrow A_{\boxed{1}}(X, Z) & , C(aX, Zc) \rightarrow C_{\boxed{1}}(X, Z) \rangle \\
\langle B(bY, dU) \rightarrow B_{\boxed{1}}(Y, U) & , D(bYd) \rightarrow D_{\boxed{1}}(Y) \rangle \\
\langle S(XYZU) \rightarrow A_{\boxed{1}}(X, Z) B_{\boxed{2}}(Y, U) , & \\
& S(XYZ) \rightarrow C_{\boxed{1}}(X, Z) D_{\boxed{2}}(Y) \rangle
\end{array}
$$

Figure 4: Sample SLCFRS for $L = \{\langle a^n b^m c^n d^m, a^n b^m d^m c^n \rangle \mid n, m > 0\}$

SLCFRS G is in *normal form* if the following two conditions hold: (a) the rank of G is at most 2 and (b) for all $r \in P$ it holds that the LHS arguments of r_s and r_t contain either terminals or variables, but no mixture of both. The grammar in Figure 4 is not in normal form.

While ITGs constrain the order of the non-terminals in the RHS of the target side to be in the same or in the reverse order compared to the non-terminals in the RHS of the source side, we do not impose such ordering constraints (on the variables) for SLCFRS. However, it is obvious that a $(2, 2_{1|1})$-SLCFRS is equivalent to an ITG of rank 2 and that a $(2, 2_{1|1})$-SLCFRS in normal form is equivalent to a NF-ITG.

2.3 Alignment Capacity

A translation unit is a maximally connected subgraph of a given alignment structure. Typically this is the smallest unit from which translation models are learned. During a synchronous derivation, we interpret simultaneously recognized terminals as aligned (Wu, 1997). They thus correspond to a translation unit. We call the synchronous derivation tree a hierarchical alignment. Many-to-many alignments are interpreted conjunctively. This means that to induce a given translation unit, a grammar has to be able to generate the complete translation unit, and not just one of the corresponding word alignments. The last point has been argued for in Søgaard and Kuhn (2009).

SLCFRS are able to induce the alignment structures under consideration (in Figure 1). This is exemplified by the rules given in Figure 5.

Clearly, there exist many different possible hierarchical alignments for a given alignment structure. The underlying constraints for the grammars in Figure 5 are (a) each translation unit is represented by

(i)

$\langle A(a) \rightarrow \varepsilon \quad , A(a) \rightarrow \varepsilon \rangle$
$\langle A(Xb) \rightarrow A_{\boxed{1}}(X) \ , A(b,Y) \rightarrow A_{\boxed{1}}(Y) \rangle$
$\langle A(Xc) \rightarrow A_{\boxed{1}}(X) \ , A(Y_1, Y_2c) \rightarrow A_{\boxed{1}}(Y_1, Y_2) \rangle$
$\langle A(Xd) \rightarrow A_{\boxed{1}}(X) \ , A(Y_1dY_2) \rightarrow A_{\boxed{1}}(Y_1, Y_2) \rangle$

(ii)

$\langle A(a) \rightarrow \varepsilon \quad , A(a_1, a_2) \rightarrow \varepsilon \rangle$
$\langle A(Xb) \rightarrow A_{\boxed{1}}(X) \ , A(Y_1b_1Y_2b_2) \rightarrow A_{\boxed{1}}(Y_1, Y_2) \rangle$
or
$\langle A(b) \rightarrow \varepsilon \quad , A(b_1, b_2) \rightarrow \varepsilon \rangle$
$\langle A(aX) \rightarrow A_{\boxed{1}}(X) \ , A(a_1Y_1a_2Y_2) \rightarrow A_{\boxed{1}}(Y_1, Y_2) \rangle$

(iii)

$\langle A(a_1, a_2) \rightarrow \varepsilon \quad , A(a) \rightarrow \varepsilon \rangle$
$\langle A(X_1bX_2) \rightarrow A_{\boxed{1}}(X_1, X_2) \ , A(b_1Yb_2) \rightarrow A_{\boxed{1}}(Y) \rangle$
or
$\langle A(b) \rightarrow \varepsilon \quad , A(b_1, b_2) \rightarrow \varepsilon \rangle$
$\langle A(a_1Xa_2) \rightarrow A_{\boxed{1}}(X) \ , A(Y_1aY_2) \rightarrow A_{\boxed{1}}(Y_1, Y_2) \rangle$

Figure 5: SLCFRS rules that induce the alignments in Figure 1. For (i) there are many other derivations possible, since there are 4! possibilities to combine the translation units in a binary way. The shown rules correspond to Figure 2(i).

exactly one rule and (b) each rule aligns exactly one translation unit and combines it with at most one already established synchronous constituent.

ITG and NF-ITG do not generate the same class of alignments (Søgaard and Wu, 2009). In parallel, a $(2, v)$-SLCFRS in normal form does not generate the same class of alignments as an unrestricted $(2, v)$-SLCFRS. Consider, for example, a discontinuous translation unit d with two gaps on the source side and a grammar G with fan-out $3_{2|1}$. G in normal form cannot induce d. In general, for generating x gaps, a fan-out of $x + 1$ is required. However, without the normal form requirement, G can possibly induce d with a rule that combines the terminals of d with the constituents that fill the gaps.

2.4 Parsing Complexity

LCFRS in normal form can be parsed in $\mathcal{O}(n^{3k})$ where k is the fan-out of the grammar (Seki et al., 1991). This result can be transferred to SLCFRS: An SLCFRS with fan-out v is essentially an LCFRS with fan-out $v + 1$. However, because of the start non-terminal S with $dim(S) = 2$, all non-terminals $A \in N$ with $dim(A) \geq 2$ and the special interpretation of the source/target side meaning that variables occur either on the source or target side but

$\langle T(\boldsymbol{\alpha_s}) \rightarrow \varepsilon \quad , T(\boldsymbol{\beta_t}) \rightarrow \varepsilon \rangle$
$\langle A(\boldsymbol{\alpha_1}) \rightarrow T_{\boxed{1}}(\boldsymbol{\alpha_1}) \quad , A(\boldsymbol{\beta_1}) \rightarrow T_{\boxed{1}}(\boldsymbol{\beta_1}) \rangle$
$\langle A(\boldsymbol{\alpha_1}) \rightarrow A_{\boxed{1}}(\boldsymbol{\alpha_2})A_{\boxed{2}}(\boldsymbol{\alpha_3}) \ , A(\boldsymbol{\beta_1}) \rightarrow A_{\boxed{1}}(\boldsymbol{\beta_2})A_{\boxed{2}}(\boldsymbol{\beta_3}) \rangle$

where $\boldsymbol{\alpha_s} \in (T_s{}^*)^{k_0}, \boldsymbol{\beta_t} \in (T_t{}^*)^{k'_0}, \boldsymbol{\alpha_i} \in (V_s{}^+)^{k_j}, \boldsymbol{\beta_i} \in (V_t{}^+)^{k'_j}$ for $0 < k_j \leq k_s, 0 < k'_j \leq k_t, 0 < i \leq 3, 0 \leq j \leq 3$

Figure 6: All-accepting SCLFRS in normal form with fan-out $v = k_s + k_t$

cannot change sides, no items that cross or involve the additional gap have to be built during parsing. Bitext parsing with SLCFRS in normal form can therefore also be performed in $\mathcal{O}(n^{3v})$ where $n = \max(n_s, n_t)$, or more specifically $\mathcal{O}(n_s^{3v_{G_s}} n_t^{3v_{G_t}})$ where n_s, n_t are the lengths of the source and target input strings respectively.

3 Empirical Investigation

Since parsing complexity with SLCFRS is determined by the fan-out v of the grammar, we conduct an investigation to find out which v would be required to fully cover the alignment configurations that occur in manually aligned parallel corpora.

3.1 Bottom-Up Hierarchical Aligner

Our study is based on *alignment validation* (Søgaard, 2010), i.e. we check whether an alignment structure can be generated by an all-accepting SLCFRS with a specific v. Such a grammar is depicted in Figure 6. Note in particular that it leaves open how to compose the yield of the LHS non-terminal from the two RHS constituents. To be able to use the grammar for parsing, one would have to spell out all combination possibilities.

Instead, we use the idea of a bottom-up hierarchical aligner (Wellington et al., 2006). It works very much like a synchronous parser, but the constraints for inferences are the word alignments and potentially other things, and not the rewriting rules of a grammar. Initial constituents are built from the word alignments, then constituents are combined with each other. The goal is to find a constituent that completely covers the input. In our case, the constraints for the hierarchical aligner come from the translation units, the fan-out $v_{k_s|k_t}$ of the simulated grammar and possibly a normal-form requirement.

We specify the hierarchical aligner in terms of a deduction system (Shieber et al., 1995). Deduction rules have the form $\frac{A_1 \ldots A_m}{B}\ C$ where $A_1 \ldots A_m$ and B are *items*, i.e. intermediate parsing results, and C is a list of conditions on $A_1 \ldots A_m$ and B. The interpretation is that if $A_1 \ldots A_m$ can be deduced and conditions C hold, then B can be deduced. Our items have the form $\langle [X_s, \boldsymbol{\rho}_s], [X_t, \boldsymbol{\rho}_t] \rangle$ where $X_s \in N_s$ and $X_t \in N_t$ of the simulated grammar. All-accepting grammars usually have only one non-terminal symbol, but we need a distinction between pre-terminal constituents T and general constituents A for simulating SLCFRS in normal form as well as the full class. $\boldsymbol{\rho}_s$ and $\boldsymbol{\rho}_t$ characterize the spans of the synchronous constituent on the source and target side respectively. We view them as bit vectors where $\boldsymbol{\rho}_s(i) = 1$ means that s_i is in the yield of X_s, and $\boldsymbol{\rho}_t(i') = 1$ that $\mathbf{t}_{i'}$ is in the yield of X_t. $\langle \mathrm{s}_{0\ldots n}, \mathbf{t}_{0\ldots n'} \rangle$ is the input sentence pair that is segmented into m disjoint translation units $\langle D_s^{(m)}, D_t^{(m)} \rangle$ based on the given word alignment structure. $D_s^{(m)}$ and $D_t^{(m)}$ are sets of word indices into s and $\mathbf{t}$ respectively. We furthermore specify some useful operations for bit vectors. The $\cup$ operator combines bit vectors of the same length to a new bit vector by an elementwise *or* operation, while the intersection $\cap$ of two bit vectors is the elementwise *and* operation. 0^l is a bit vector $\boldsymbol{\rho}$ such that $\boldsymbol{\rho}(i) = 0$ for all $0 \leq i \leq l$. The function $b(\boldsymbol{\rho})$ returns the number of blocks of $\boldsymbol{\rho}$, i.e. the number of continuous sequences of 1s in $\boldsymbol{\rho}$.

Figure 7 shows the deduction rules of the hierarchical aligner that simulate an all-accepting SLCFRS in normal form. *Scan* builds T items from translation units, *Unary* creates A items from T items, and *Binary* combines two A items to a larger A item. Via the side conditions, A items are only created if they respect the specified fan-out $v_{k_s|k_t}$ of the all-accepting grammar. If the hierarchical aligner finds an A item that spans $\langle \mathbf{s}, \mathbf{t} \rangle$, the alignment structure of $\langle \mathbf{s}, \mathbf{t} \rangle$ is valid, i.e. can be induced by an SLCFRS in normal form with fan-out $v_{k_s|k_t}$.

Since we are also interested in the empirical alignment capacity of SLCFRS without normal-form restriction, we present an extended deduction system in Figure 8. The additional rules lead to the simulation of an SLCFRS of rank 2 where terminals and variables can be combined in the arguments of the LHS non-terminals of the rewriting rules. Note in particular that the generation of T items is not constrained by a maximally allowed $v_{k_s|k_t}$.

For the computation of the items, we use standard chart parsing techniques, maintaining a chart and an agenda.

3.2 Data

We use manually aligned parallel corpora for our study.[2] Data sets that have already been previously used in similar experiments, e.g. in Wellington et al. (2006), Søgaard and Wu (2009), and Søgaard (2010), are those from Martin et al. (2005) for English-Romanian and English-Hindi, the English-French data from Mihalcea and Pedersen (2003), the Europarl data set described in Graça et al. (2008) for the six combinations of English, French, Portuguese and Spanish, the English-German Europarl data that was created for Padó and Lapata (2006), and data sets with Danish as the source language that are part of the Parole corpus of the Copenhagen Dependency Treebank (Buch-Kromann et al., 2009).

We furthermore perform our study on data sets that, to the best of our knowledge, have not been evaluated in a similar setting before. Those are English-Swedish gold alignments documented in Holmqvist and Ahrenberg (2011), the English-Inuktitut data used in Martin et al. (2005), more English-German data[3], the English-Spanish data set in Lambert et al. (2005) and English-Dutch alignments that are part of the Dutch Parallel Corpus (Macken, 2010). Characteristics about the data sets are presented in the last columns of Table 1.

3.3 Method

We apply the bottom-up hierarchical alignment algorithm in various configurations to each manually aligned sentence pair. If a goal item is found, the alignment structure can be induced with the formalism in question. We measure the number of sentence pairs for which a hierarchical alignment was reached over the total number of sentence pairs. Søgaard (2010) refers to this as *alignment reachability*, which is the inverse of *parse failure rate* (Wellington et al., 2006).

[2] Whenever there are sure (S) and possible (P) alignments annotated, we use both.

[3] By T. Schoenemann, from `http://user.phil-fak.uni-duesseldorf.de/~tosch/downloads.html`

Scan: $\dfrac{}{\langle [T, \boldsymbol{\rho}_s], [T, \boldsymbol{\rho}_t] \rangle}$ a translation unit $\langle D_s, D_t \rangle$
where $\boldsymbol{\rho}_s(i) = 1$ if $i \in D_s$, otherwise $\boldsymbol{\rho}_s(i) = 0$, and $\boldsymbol{\rho}_t(i') = 1$ if $i' \in D_t$, otherwise $\boldsymbol{\rho}_t(i') = 0$

Unary: $\dfrac{\langle [T, \boldsymbol{\rho}_s], [T, \boldsymbol{\rho}_t] \rangle}{\langle [A, \boldsymbol{\rho}_s], [A, \boldsymbol{\rho}_t] \rangle} \quad b(\boldsymbol{\rho}_s) \leq k_s, b(\boldsymbol{\rho}_t) \leq k_t$

Binary: $\dfrac{\langle [A, \boldsymbol{\rho}_s^1], [A, \boldsymbol{\rho}_t^1] \rangle, \langle [A, \boldsymbol{\rho}_s^2], [A, \boldsymbol{\rho}_t^2] \rangle}{\langle [A, \boldsymbol{\rho}_s^3], [A, \boldsymbol{\rho}_t^3] \rangle} \quad \boldsymbol{\rho}_s^1 \cap \boldsymbol{\rho}_s^2 = 0^n, \boldsymbol{\rho}_t^1 \cap \boldsymbol{\rho}_t^2 = 0^{n'}, b(\boldsymbol{\rho}_s^3) \leq k_s, b(\boldsymbol{\rho}_t^3) \leq k_t$
where $\boldsymbol{\rho}_s^3 = \boldsymbol{\rho}_s^1 \cup \boldsymbol{\rho}_s^2$ and $\boldsymbol{\rho}_t^3 = \boldsymbol{\rho}_t^1 \cup \boldsymbol{\rho}_t^2$

Goal: $\langle [A, \boldsymbol{\rho}_s], [A, \boldsymbol{\rho}_t] \rangle$
where $\boldsymbol{\rho}_s(i) = 1$ for all $0 \leq i \leq n$ and $\boldsymbol{\rho}_t(i') = 1$ for all $0 \leq i' \leq n'$

Figure 7: CYK deduction system for an all-accepting SLCFRS in normal form with fan-out $v_{k_s|k_t}$

UnaryMixed: $\dfrac{\langle [T, \boldsymbol{\rho}_s^T], [T, \boldsymbol{\rho}_t^T] \rangle, \langle [A, \boldsymbol{\rho}_s^A], [A, \boldsymbol{\rho}_t^A] \rangle}{\langle [A, \boldsymbol{\rho}_s], [A, \boldsymbol{\rho}_t] \rangle} \quad \boldsymbol{\rho}_s^T \cap \boldsymbol{\rho}_s^A = 0^n, \boldsymbol{\rho}_t^T \cap \boldsymbol{\rho}_t^A = 0^{n'}, b(\boldsymbol{\rho}_s) \leq k_s, b(\boldsymbol{\rho}_t) \leq k_t$
where $\boldsymbol{\rho}_s = \boldsymbol{\rho}_s^T \cup \boldsymbol{\rho}_s^A$ and $\boldsymbol{\rho}_t = \boldsymbol{\rho}_t^T \cup \boldsymbol{\rho}_t^A$

BinaryMixed: $\dfrac{\langle [T, \boldsymbol{\rho}_s^T], [T, \boldsymbol{\rho}_t^T] \rangle, \langle [A, \boldsymbol{\rho}_s^1], [A, \boldsymbol{\rho}_t^1] \rangle, \langle [A, \boldsymbol{\rho}_s^2], [A, \boldsymbol{\rho}_t^2] \rangle}{\langle [A, \boldsymbol{\rho}_s^3], [A, \boldsymbol{\rho}_t^3] \rangle} \quad \begin{array}{c} \boldsymbol{\rho}_s^T \cap \boldsymbol{\rho}_s^1 = 0^n, \boldsymbol{\rho}_s^1 \cap \boldsymbol{\rho}_s^2 = 0^n, \boldsymbol{\rho}_s^2 \cap \boldsymbol{\rho}_s^T = 0^n, \\ \boldsymbol{\rho}_t^T \cap \boldsymbol{\rho}_t^1 = 0^{n'}, \boldsymbol{\rho}_t^1 \cap \boldsymbol{\rho}_t^2 = 0^{n'}, \boldsymbol{\rho}_t^2 \cap \boldsymbol{\rho}_t^T = 0^{n'}, \\ b(\boldsymbol{\rho}_s^3) \leq k_s, b(\boldsymbol{\rho}_t^3) \leq k_t \end{array}$
where $\boldsymbol{\rho}_s^3 = \boldsymbol{\rho}_s^T \cup \boldsymbol{\rho}_s^1 \cup \boldsymbol{\rho}_s^2$ and $\boldsymbol{\rho}_t^3 = \boldsymbol{\rho}_t^T \cup \boldsymbol{\rho}_t^1 \cup \boldsymbol{\rho}_t^2$

Figure 8: Additional inference rules for the deduction system in Figure 7 for simulating an SLCFRS of rank 2 without normal form restriction.

		SLCFRS				Søgaard (2010)		**Data**			
		NF		$u = 2$							
		$v = 2_{1\|1}$ = NF-ITG	$v = 4_{2\|2}$	$v = 2_{1\|1}$ = ITG	$v = 4_{2\|2}$	NF-ITG	ITG	#SPs	min	med	max
	en-ro (30)	45.07	**97.85**	95.07	**100.00**	-	-	447	2|2	20|19	96|94
Martin	en-hi (40)	82.73	**100.00**	96.36	$^{1\|2}_{2\|1}$**100.00**	-	-	115	1|1	10|12	45|58
	en-iu (40)	40.66	**95.60**	100.00	**100.00**	-	-	100	10|3	26|10	79|26
Pado	en-de (15)	73.74	**100.00**	94.41	$^{1\|2}$**100.00**	38.97	45.13	987	5|5	24|23	40|40
Mihal.	en-fr	67.56	**98.88**	95.30	**100.00**	*76.98	*81.75	447	2|2	16|17	30|30
	en-fr	73.00	**100.00**	95.00	$^{1\|2}$**100.00**	65.00	68.00	100	4|4	11|13	14|21
	en-pt	76.00	**100.00**	98.00	$^{1\|2}_{2\|1}$**100.00**	65.00	67.00	100	4|3	11|12	14|21
Graça	en-es	82.00	**100.00**	96.00	$^{1\|2}_{2\|1}$**100.00**	73.00	74.00	100	4|4	11|11	14|24
	pt-fr	73.00	**97.00**	92.00	$^{1\|2}$**100.00**	63.00	63.00	100	3|4	12|13	21|21
	pt-es	90.00	**99.00**	99.00	$^{1\|2}_{2\|1}$**100.00**	80.00	81.00	100	3|4	12|11	21|24
	es-fr	74.00	**100.00**	91.00	$^{1\|2}$**100.00**	68.00	68.00	100	4|4	11|13	24|21
	da-en (25)	72.90	**98.93**	97.80	**100.00**	-	-	5464	1|1	16|17	89|98
CDT	da-de (25)	64.87	**98.42**	94.94	$^{1\|2}_{2\|1}$**100.00**	*47.62	*49.35	449	1|1	17|18	75|74
	da-es (25)	66.61	**97.68**	97.50	**100.00**	*30.68	*35.54	807	1|1	16|18	78|97
	da-it (25)	69.01	**97.65**	97.95	**100.00**	*60.00	*60.00	1514	1|1	16|19	78|268
Holmqv.	en-sv (30)	82.83	**99.78**	95.60	**100.00**	-	-	1164	1|1	21|19	40|40
Schoen.	en-de (40)	29.15	**94.74**	76.11	**100.00**	-	-	300	1|1	21|22	77|79
Lambert	en-es (40)	47.15	**97.83**	94.85	**100.00**	-	-	500	4|4	26|27	90|99
Macken	en-nl (30)	57.14	**98.86**	94.86	**100.00**	-	-	699	1|1	20|19	107|105

Table 1: Alignment reachability scores of our experiments and those of Søgaard (2010), plus characteristics of the data sets. The numbers in parentheses are the sentence length cut-offs used in our experiments. The results marked with * are not directly comparable to ours because different versions of the data sets were used.

3.4 Results

Table 1 shows the results. It confirmes that NF-ITG is not capable of generating the majority of alignment configurations. However, when allowing discontinuous constituents with maximally two blocks on each side ($v = 4_{2|2}$), NF-SLCFRS induces all alignments present in six of the data sets, and reaches scores > 97 for the other data sets, except two of them for which scores are still > 94.7.

For grammars without normal-form constraint, alignment reachability is generally higher. We tested grammars of rank 2 and found that over 90% of the sentence pairs in each data set can be induced without the necessity of discontinuous constituents (except data set *Schoen.*). Such grammars roughly correspond to successfully applied translation models, e.g. in Hiero (Chiang, 2007). Nevertheless, our experiments show that the gold alignments contain a proportion of structures that cannot be generated by ITGs. With a $(2, 4_{2|2})$-SLCFRS, all occurring alignment configurations are captured. For some data sets, a fan-out of 3 is enough to induce all alignments. This is indicated by $^{1|2}$ and $_{2|1}$.

Going back to grammars in normal form, the sentence pairs that cannot be induced with a grammar of fan-out $4_{2|2}$ all display translation units that require three (or very rarely four) blocks on at least the source or the target side. An interesting observation is that only the English-Inuktitut data can nevertheless be generated with fan-out 4, by distributing the allowed discontinuity unequally: with a NF-SLCFRS with fan-out $4_{3|1}$, the alignment reachability is 100. This is not surprising given the fact that Inuktitut is a polysynthetic language.

Previous results by Søgaard (2010) concerning the coverage of ITG and NF-ITG on hand-aligned data, repeated for convenience in Table 1, are much lower than ours and therefore present a highly distorted picture concerning the empirical need of discontinuous constituents. This is due to the fact that the implementation[4] used for the experiments handles unaligned words incorrectly. They are added deterministically to the first constituent that encounters them, which leads to false negatives as further explained in Figure 9. After fixing this issue, the same results as for NF-SLCFRS with $v = 2_{1|1}$ are obtained. Another problem of the implementation concerns discontinuous translation units. Søgaard's alignment validation returns *false* if the words in the gap are aligned, although such configurations are induced by unrestricted ITG, see Søgaard and Wu (2009, Section 3.2.1).

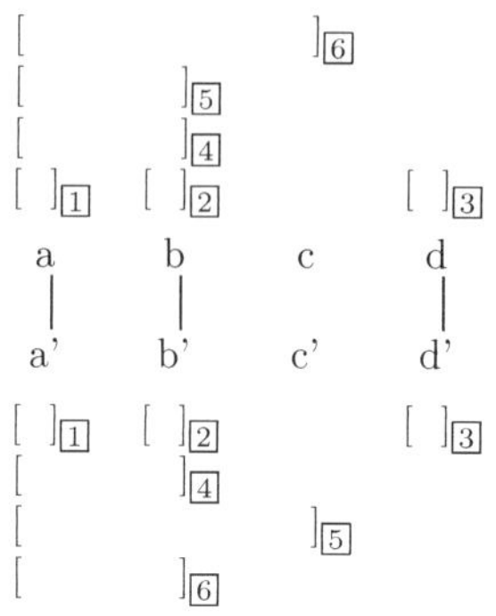

Figure 9: Synchronous ITG parse chart provided by the implementation from Søgaard (2010): *c* "belongs to" constituent 6 while *c'* "belongs to" constituent 5. When trying to combine 4 and 3, *c* and *c'* are not considered as unaligned because they are already part of a constituent, and neither 5 nor 6 can be combined with 3 without creating a discontinuous constituent. The algorithm cannot find a larger continuous constituent, the alignment validation therefore returns *false*. However, this simple alignment structure lies within the power of NF-ITG and ITG.

4 Discussion

Our experiments show that by moving from synchronous grammars with only continuous constituents to grammars that allow two blocks per constituent, (almost) all manual alignments can be generated, depending on whether the normal-form is enforced or not. Given the parsing complexity that comes with allowing discontinuities, this is a promising finding since it has already been shown for monolingual parsing that restricting the fan-out to 2 drastically reduces parsing times (Maier et al., 2012). In the future, we might also investigate whether refraining from ill-nested structures (Maier and Lichte, 2011) is a reasonable option for tree-based machine translation in order to reduce complexity (Gómez-Rodríguez et al., 2010).

Even though bitext parsing complexity for SLCFRS is prohibitively high, we expect that, given the techniques that have been developed for translation with SCFG, SLCFRS finds its application as a

[4] http://cst.dk/anders/itg-search.html

translation model. In practice, only source side parsing is performed for translation and various pruning methods are applied to reduce the search space (e.g. in Chiang (2005), Yamada and Knight (2002) and many others).

It should also be mentioned that it is not clear yet how alignment reachability scores relate to machine translation quality and evaluation. We can nevertheless infer from the presented results that what is considered as translationally equivalent by the annotators of the data sets and their guidelines is beyond the search space of SCFG. A supplementary study could furthermore investigate translation unit error rates (Søgaard and Kuhn, 2009) for the data sets, under the assumption of a hierarchical SLCFRS alignment with a specific fan-out.

5 Related Work

Our empirical investigation extends previous studies, and thus provides new insights. Both Wellington et al. (2006) and Søgaard (2010) use a bottom-up hierarchical alignment algorithm with the goal of investigating the alignment complexity of manually aligned parallel corpora. Søgaard (2010) is however only interested in the alignment reachability of ITG and NF-ITG, and nothing beyond. We have furthermore revealed that the presented results underestimate the alignment capacity of ITG and NF-ITG.

The study of Wellington et al. (2006) is very similar to ours in that the number of blocks in discontinuous constituents that are required for hierarchical alignment are investigated. The word alignments are however treated disjunctively, which means that in the case of n-to-m alignments with $n, m \geq 1$, it is enough to induce one of the involved alignments. With this methodology a large class of discontinuities we are interested in, e.g. cross-serial discontinuous translation units, is ignored. The failure rates they present are therefore much lower than ours. Wellington et al. (2006) also show that when constraining synchronous derivations by monolingual syntactic parse trees on the source and/or target side, allowing discontinuous constituents becomes even more important for inducing gold alignments.

We are of course not the first to propose a translation model that is expressive enough to induce the alignments in question in Figure 1. Following up on a translation model proposed by Simard et al. (2005), Galley and Manning (2010) extend the phrase-based approach in that they allow for discontinuous phrase pairs. Their system outperforms a phrase-based system and a system based on SCFG of rank 2. In a way, our proposal to use SLCFRS is the syntax-based counterpart to their approach. Methods to integrate linguistic constituency information into the so far only formal tree-based approach can be directly transferred from the SCFG-based approaches to SLCFRS. In constrast, it is not obvious how to include such information into the phrase-based systems.

Søgaard (2008) proposes to use an even more expressive formalism than LCFRS, namely range concatenation grammar, and to exploit its ability to copy substrings during the derivation. The downsides of this approach are already mentioned in Søgaard and Kuhn (2009); for example, no tight probability estimation is possible for such a grammar.

The necessity of going towards mildly context-sensitive formalisms for translation modeling has also been advocated by Melamed (Melamed et al., 2004; Melamed, 2004). This step was however not motivated by the induction of specific complex translation units, but rather by the general observation that discontinuous constituents are necessary for synchronous derivations using linguistically motivated grammars. Discontinuous constituents also emerge when binarizing synchronous grammars of continuous yields with rank ≥ 4 (Melamed, 2003; Rambow and Satta, 1999).

6 Conclusion

Motivated by the finding that synchronous CFG cannot induce certain alignment configurations, we suggest to use synchronous LCFRS instead, which allows for discontinuities. Even though our empirical investigation shows that with exclusively continuous derivations more manual alignments can be captured than previously reported, there are still many aligned sentence pairs that can only be generated when setting the fan-out of the translation grammar to > 2. It remains to determine how such more accurate and more expressive models relate to translation quality.

Acknowledgments

I would like to thank Laura Kallmeyer and Wolfgang Maier for discussions and comments, the reviewers for their suggestions, Anders Søgaard for discussions concerning ITG and his implementation, and Zdeněk Žabokrtský for helping with the CDT data. This research was funded by the German Research Foundation as part of the project *Grammar Formalisms beyond Context-Free Grammars and their use for Machine Learning Tasks*.

References

Pierre Boullier. 1998. Proposal for a Natural Language Processing syntactic backbone. Technical Report 3342, INRIA.

Matthias Buch-Kromann, Iørn Korzen, and Henrik Høeg Müller. 2009. Uncovering the lost structure of translations with parallel treebanks. *Copenhagen Studies in Language*, 38:199–224.

David Chiang. 2005. A hierarchical phrase-based model for statistical machine translation. In *Proceedings of the 43rd Annual Meeting on Association for Computational Linguistics*, pages 263–270.

David Chiang. 2007. Hierarchical phrase-based translation. *Computational Linguistics*, 33(2):201–228.

Kilian Evang and Laura Kallmeyer. 2011. PLCFRS parsing of English discontinuous constituents. In *Proceedings of the 12th International Conference on Parsing Technologies (IWPT)*, pages 104–116.

Michel Galley and Christopher D. Manning. 2010. Accurate non-hierarchical phrase-based translation. In *Human Language Technologies: The 2010 Annual Conference of the North American Chapter of the Association for Computational Linguistics*, pages 966–974.

Carlos Gómez-Rodríguez, Marco Kuhlmann, and Giorgio Satta. 2010. Efficient parsing of well-nested Linear Context-Free Rewriting Systems. In *Human Language Technologies: The 2010 Annual Conference of the North American Chapter of the Association for Computational Linguistics*, pages 276–284.

João de Almeida Varelas Graça, Joana Paulo Pardal, Luísa Coheur, and Diamantino António Caseiro. 2008. Building a golden collection of parallel multi-language word alignment. In *The 6th International Conference on Language Resources and Evaluation (LREC08)*.

Hieu Hoang and Philipp Koehn. 2010. Improved translation with source syntax labels. In *Proceedings of the Joint Fifth Workshop on Statistical Machine Translation and MetricsMATR*, pages 409–417. Association for Computational Linguistics.

Maria Holmqvist and Lars Ahrenberg. 2011. A gold standard for English–Swedish word alignment. In *Proceedings of the 18th Nordic Conference of Computational Linguistics NODALIDA 2011*, pages 106–113.

Laura Kallmeyer and Wolfgang Maier. 2013. Data-driven parsing using Probabilistic Linear Context-Free Rewriting Systems. *Computational Linguistics*, 39(1). Accepted for publication.

Philipp Koehn, Franz Josef Och, and Daniel Marcu. 2003. Statistical phrase-based translation. In *Proceedings of the 2003 Conference of the North American Chapter of the Association for Computational Linguistics on Human Language Technology*, pages 48–54. Association for Computational Linguistics.

Marco Kuhlmann and Giorgio Satta. 2009. Treebank grammar techniques for non-projective dependency parsing. In *Proceedings of the 12th Conference of the European Chapter of the Association for Computational Linguistics (EACL)*, pages 478–486.

Patrik Lambert, Adrià Gispert, Rafael Banchs, and José B. Mariño. 2005. Guidelines for word alignment evaluation and manual alignment. *Language Resources and Evaluation*, 39:267–285.

Lieve Macken. 2010. An annotation scheme and gold standard for Dutch-English word alignment. In *Proceedings of the Seventh International Conference on Language Resources and Evaluation (LREC'10)*.

Wolfgang Maier and Timm Lichte. 2011. Characterizing discontinuity in constituent treebanks. In *Formal Grammer 2009, Revised Selected Papers*, volume 5591 of *LNAI*. Springer.

Wolfgang Maier, Miriam Kaeshammer, and Laura Kallmeyer. 2012. Data-driven PLCFRS parsing revisited: Restricting the fan-out to two. In *Proceedings of the Eleventh International Conference on Tree Adjoining Grammars and Related Formalisms (TAG+11)*.

Wolfgang Maier. 2010. Direct parsing of discontinuous constituents in German. In *Proceedings of the NAACL HLT 2010 First Workshop on Statistical Parsing of Morphologically-Rich Languages*.

Joel Martin, Rada Mihalca, and Ted Pedersen. 2005. Word alignment for languages with scarce resources. In *ACL Workshop on Building and Using Parallel Texts*.

I. Dan Melamed, Giorgio Satta, and Benjamin Wellington. 2004. Generalized multitext grammars. In *Proceedings of the 42nd Annual Conference of the Association for Computational Linguistics (ACL)*.

I. Dan Melamed. 2003. Multitext grammars and synchronous parsers. In *Proceedings of the 2003 Con-*

ference of the North American Chapter of the Association for Computational Linguistics on Human Language Technology, pages 79–86.

I. Dan Melamed. 2004. Statistical machine translation by parsing. In *Proceedings of the 42nd Annual Conference of the Association for Computational Linguistics (ACL)*.

Rada Mihalcea and Ted Pedersen. 2003. An evaluation exercise for word alignment. In *Proceedings of the HLT-NAACL 2003 Workshop on Building and Using Parallel Texts: Data Driven Machine Translation and Beyond*, pages 1–10.

Sebastian Padó and Mirella Lapata. 2006. Optimal constituent alignment with edge covers for semantic projection. In *Proceedings of the 21st International Conference on Computational Linguistics and 44th Annual Meeting of the ACL*, pages 1161–1168.

Owen Rambow and Giorgio Satta. 1999. Independent parallelism in finite copying parallel rewriting systems. *Theoretical Computer Science*, 223(1-2):87–120.

Giorgio Satta and Enoch Peserico. 2005. Some computational complexity results for synchronous context-free grammars. In *Proceedings of Human Language Technology Conference and Conference on Empirical Methods in Natural Language Processing (HLT/EMNLP)*, pages 803–810.

Hiroyuki Seki, Takashi Matsumura, Mamoru Fujii, and Tadao Kasami. 1991. On Multiple Context-Free Grammars. *Theoretical Computer Science*, 88(2):191–229.

Stuart M. Shieber, Yves Schabes, and Fernando C. N. Pereira. 1995. Principles and implementation of deductive parsing. *Journal of Logic Programming*, 24(1&2):3–36.

Michel Simard, Nicola Cancedda, Bruno Cavestro, Marc Dymetman, Eric Gaussier, Cyril Goutte, Kenji Yamada, Philippe Langlais, and Arne Mauser. 2005. Translating with non-contiguous phrases. In *Proceedings of Human Language Technology Conference and Conference on Empirical Methods in Natural Language Processing (HLT/EMNLP)*, pages 755–762.

Anders Søgaard and Jonas Kuhn. 2009. Empirical lower bounds on alignment error rates in syntax-based machine translation. In *Proceedings of the Third Workshop on Syntax and Structure in Statistical Translation (SSST '09)*. Association for Computational Linguistics.

Anders Søgaard and Dekai Wu. 2009. Empirical lower bounds on translation unit error rate for the full class of inversion transduction grammars. In *Proceedings of the 11th International Conference on Parsing Technologies*, pages 33–36.

Anders Søgaard. 2008. Range concatenation grammars for translation. In *Proceedings of Coling 2008: Companion volume: Posters*.

Anders Søgaard. 2010. Can inversion transduction grammars generate hand alignments? In *Proccedings of the 14th Annual Conference of the European Association for Machine Translation (EAMT)*.

Andreas van Cranenburgh. 2012. Efficient parsing with Linear Context-Free Rewriting Systems. In *Proceedings of the 13th Conference of the European Chapter of the Association for Computational Linguistics*.

K. Vijay-Shanker, David Weir, and Aravind K. Joshi. 1987. Characterizing structural descriptions used by various formalisms. In *Proceedings of the 25th Annual Meeting of the Association for Computational Linguistics*.

David Weir. 1988. *Characterizing Mildly Context-Sensitive Grammar Formalisms*. Ph.D. thesis, University of Pennsylviania, Philadelphia, PA.

Benjamin Wellington, Sonjia Waxmonsky, and I. Dan Melamed. 2006. Empirical lower bounds on the complexity of translational equivalence. In *Proceedings of the 21st International Conference on Computational Linguistics and 44th Annual Meeting of the Association for Computational Linguistics*, pages 977–984.

Dekai Wu. 1997. Stochastic inversion transduction grammars and bilingual parsing of parallel corpora. *Computational linguistics*, 23(3):377–403.

Kenji Yamada and Kevin Knight. 2002. A decoder for syntax-based statistical MT. In *Proceedings of 40th Annual Meeting of the Association for Computational Linguistics*.

Andreas Zollmann and Ashish Venugopal. 2006. Syntax augmented machine translation via chart parsing. In *Proceedings of the Workshop on Statistical Machine Translation, HLT/NAACL*.

Author Index

Addanki, Karteek, 48

Carpuat, Marine, 1

Freitag, Markus, 29

Herrmann, Teresa, 39
Huck, Matthias, 29

Kaeshammer, Miriam, 68

Maillette de Buy Wenniger, Gideon, 19, 58

Ney, Hermann, 29
Niehues, Jan, 39

Saers, Markus, 48
Sima'an, Khalil, 19, 58
Singh, Thoudam Doren, 11

Vilar, David, 29

Waibel, Alex, 39
Wu, Dekai, 48